Make Millions Selling on QVC

INSIDER SECRETS TO LAUNCHING
YOUR PRODUCT ON TELEVISION AND
TRANSFORMING YOUR BUSINESS
(AND LIFE) FOREVER

Nick Romer

John Wiley & Sons, Inc.

Published by John Wiley & Sons, Inc., Hoboken, New Jersey.
Published simultaneously in Canada.

For general information on our other products and services or for technical
support, please contact our Customer Care Department within the United States at
(800) 762-2974, outside the United States at (317) 572-3993 or fax (317) 572-4002.

Wiley also publishes its books in a variety of electronic formats. Some content that
appears in print may not be available in electronic formats. For more information
about Wiley products, visit our Web site at www.wiley.com.

Library of Congress Cataloging-in-Publication Data:
Romer, Nick.
    Make millions selling on QVC : insider secrets to launching your product on
television and transforming your business (and life) forever / Nick Romer.
        p. cm.
    Includes index.
    ISBN 978-0-470-22645-2 (cloth)
        1. QVC (Firm)   2. Telemarketing.   3. Teleshopping.   4. Cable
television advertising.   I. Title.
    HF5415.1265.R67 2008
    658.8'72—dc22
                                                            2007031888

Printed in the United States of America
10   9   8   7   6   5   4   3   2   1

For Joella, Ava, Nicholas, and Madelyn.
The love that lights the way.

Contents

Acknowledgments

I am grateful for many amazing people in my life who have all been instrumental in illuminating the path and keeping the foundation of my business and life endeavors intact and upright.

First and foremost, Joella, my love. Thank you for listening to my dreams with or without the spoken words and for believing in me unconditionally.

To Marina, you are a great sister, thanks for always coming to my games and for being there in every other way throughout the years.

When I first thought I could launch a business and create an assembly line in my small condominium, my dear friends Brian and Diana Urbanski immediately offered the large basement of their home along with their willing hands for our countless packing parties. Their generosity and true friendship is something I will remain grateful for and will never forget.

To Rich Ennis and Frank Montemurro—thanks for taking the meeting and for all the guidance thereafter. Paul Haviland and Sergio Acle, true friends and believers, thanks for your constant interest, insights, and encouragement. Thank you Herb Niemi for great advice and manufacturing support throughout the years and Joyce Krompegel for keeping it all going in so many ways.

Starr Hall—I am grateful for your friendship and your nonstop pillar of positive get-it-done-and-I'll-make-it-happen support and inspiration. You are perfect in every way.

And to Alisha Wright. Thank you for your endless generosity and friendship—just one phone call and see what happened. To Debra Englander and Stacey Small at Wiley, thank you for your insights and continued support.

I am also grateful to many others including Bill Wright, Neal Inscoe, Susan Stewart, Cindy Zontek, Patti Goodyear, Suzanne

viii   **Acknowledgments**

Runyan, Olga Romer, Miklos Homolka, Tom Annerino, Barbara Eastwick, Alicia Sheerin, Louie Ponstingel, Melinda Oakes, and also all the great people at QVC in front of the camera, behind the camera, and operating behind the scenes.

In the beginning, the middle, and the present, Divine Guidance brought it and us all together.

Introduction

I just might be the person sitting next to you on the train as you read this. I might be the man next to you at our children's school function. I might be the man you see pumping his own gas at the gas station as you pass by. For I am an everyday person, with everyday needs not unlike any of your own, and I do everyday things with my family and friends, just like any other person.

One day though, in the course of a regular day, a remarkable thing happened to me. I invented something. It all started when a friend asked me to go to lunch with her. During the course of lunch she pulled out a shoebox filled with colorful envelopes. I have a very diverse background, so it's not uncommon for one of my friends to seek me out for advice.

The envelopes were quite different. Other than the hand-decorated envelopes I used to receive from one of my high school friends after we went off to college, I had seen colored envelopes only around the holidays.

The envelopes she showed me that day weren't just a solid color, though. They contained popular cartoon characters and other fun images. She was thinking about starting a business and wanted to know my opinion about whether she could sell the envelopes she had made.

The problem with her envelopes was that they contained characters that were trademarked and protected by law. It would involve getting in contact with the various companies and entering into a licensing agreement, a process a little more involved then going to the local church fair and setting up a table.

But as she was putting them away she said, "That's okay; it takes me forever to make one anyway." And in a flash, I saw a shape in my mind's eye. It looked like a baseball diamond with a rectangle cut out of the middle. The image wouldn't go away.

After I came home, the shape was still haunting me, so I made one out of cardboard. I literally cut it out of a manila folder and began tearing up whatever magazines and paper were near me to see if it would work. When I obliterated my immediate supply, I turned to the corner of the living room, where my roommate had piled magazines from various subscriptions. I couldn't resist. In seconds I was at it again, cranking out unique envelope after unique envelope until I could hear the chirp of morning birds and saw the sun coming through the windows. By this time I had made about five hundred amazing one-of-a-kind envelopes. I was addicted. I needed more paper. In the kitchen I found some old newspapers and an old calendar and got back to business.

When my roommate woke up that morning and came into the living room he found me sitting at the table still going at it, a mess of shredded paper in my midst. Rubbing his eyes, he took it all in. As he looked around the room he spotted the empty corner and asked, "Where are my magazines?" I smiled a mile wide and handed him my colorful stack of envelopes. "You're looking at them. Aren't they cool?" I said. He smiled back, nodding his head, understanding fully what I had done. He totally got it, and didn't mind at all. We still laugh about it to this day.

The tool was magic. Soon I had some made out of plastic and started selling them at a nearby shopping mall, along with my friend who I had had lunch with that fateful day. Then one day soon after, another friend told me to go to the local rubber stamp store. I didn't know what my friend was talking about. I had never heard of a rubber stamp store before, but apparently there was one in my town, so off I went.

The store owner, Helen, was amazed. She said she wanted to stock them, but not with all the paper and stickers I had by then put in a box to be included with each one. Then, she had a thought. She was having a small open house that weekend in her store and wanted me to come. She told me, "Bring as many of those plastic things as you can."

I showed up with sixty five. I was led to a room packed with eager rubber stampers, all women. I looked at Helen and wondered aloud if I was in the wrong room. She said, no, they were there to see me.

She explained that not too many men show up to these things unless they're dragged.

This I understood all too well. I didn't know a thing about this rubber stamping thing—or crafts, for that matter—and seeing this room filled with what I thought were crazed women, I wasn't sure I was in the right place. I was, after all, interested in sports and the normal guy things, not paper crafts and rubber stamping.

When the time came, I nervously began my demonstration. With the first tear of paper, one of the onlookers yelled, "How much?" I hesitated. I was unraveling as fast as a ball of yarn in the claws of a skilled kitten. I was just getting started. I remember thinking to myself, what did I get myself into? I continued working the magical template and ignored the question.

Then another yelled again, "How much?" I thought I was being heckled. This time I answered, "They're five dollars each but I only have 65 of them with me." And with that it was as if I was one of the Beatles. There was a sudden rush of women hurling themselves in my direction. In a matter of seconds, I found myself stuffed in the corner of the room until Helen rushed to my rescue and told the ladies to settle down, there were enough for everyone.

I ended up calling my two little pieces of plastic The Kreate-a-lope® Envelope Maker. It is a template system that shows anyone how to make an envelope out of any kind of paper in seconds. I bill it as The Fastest Envelope Maker on the Planet!™ And it really is. I can make an envelope in 11 seconds!

At the time I was working in the field of energy conservation for a subsidiary of ALCOA, the Aluminum Company of America. We would go into commercial buildings and retrofit their lighting and heating systems with new technology and, in the process, save the occupants as much as 70 percent on their utility bills. I had recently started a new sales territory for the company in the Washington, D.C./Baltimore area.

Additionally, I was flipping real estate on the side. I would find dilapidated homes and refurbish them to either rent or sell. Since then, and much in part to the recent real estate boom, this form has been popularized with more than one television show on the subject.

My regular job was like any other. It paid the bills. I felt it was important and that I was contributing to society, but after seven years I was ready for something else, and the envelope maker came along at the right time for me to make a change. Out of the blue one day, I called my boss and gave my two weeks notice. He asked me what I was going to do, and I said I didn't really know. But I knew I was very interested in seeing what the Kreate-a-lope® had in store for me.

Somewhere before the craziness started, a patent was filed and subsequently issued in twelve months, which is quick. I was told there was nothing like it.

So once I quit my job and turned my focus on my two little pieces of plastic, I found myself in an industry far from my own. I was clueless as to what steps to take in order to share my idea with many. I had hundreds of questions about the marketing process, retailing, pricing, manufacturing, and everything else one could possibly think of the first time they ever develop an idea. The most pressing question of all, though, was where to begin.

If you have the same questions, you're in luck, because this book contains information about what many believe to be a high-speed rocket to launching a new or existing product. It contains answers to many of the questions I had and have road-tested since the beginning to great success.

My little template was not an earth-shattering invention like the television, microchip, or the light bulb, but a simple little tool that could be used by a very small part of the population. It was a first for me in many respects, and I bumbled along with my innovative idea like the proverbial fish out of water.

A short time into this journey, another remarkable thing happened. I call it divine intervention, or perhaps—with respect for those who might be sensitive to such a description—a turn of synchronistic events. But no matter how I describe the path of destiny that seemed to open before me, the end result was that I went from being confused about where to begin to sitting in front of buyers for a then-fledgling television home-shopping channel called QVC.

The beauty of getting on QVC was that I could bypass most of the ground-level activities involved with launching a product, and the grueling learning curve of how to do it, and go straight to the top—direct to market in a plain brown box—broadcasting to millions.

That day changed the course of my life. This story is the testimonial of how an average person with a great idea and limited resources—but just the right opportunity—can make millions of dollars on QVC. This story is about what to do to get on, stay on, and change your business and life forever by getting you and your products in front of millions of eager people waiting for your idea in the comfort of their own homes.

This story is a billion-dollar inside look at QVC, the largest television retailer in the world. The information within can be used by anyone in any industry in any facet, whether an inventor, entrepreneur, salesperson, large or small corporation, mother of three asked to demonstrate a product for her inventor neighbor, or anyone preparing for their first meeting with the kingpin of the home shopping industry.

If the greatest product in the world were being shown in the middle of the woods, would anyone buy it? But bring in the cameras, pipe in 87 million viewers, and even the smallest business with the smallest innovative idea in the world can find success.

I did it. So can you. Here's an anatomical view of how.

CHAPTER 1

How a Niche Product Generated $441,158.40 in Ten Minutes

Host: "Okay, we're live with our next guest, Nick Romer . . . and he brings us a brand new product today. . . ." Bang! The demonstration. The back and forth chatter. The camera angles. Hand-held camera coming close. An off-stage clatter of pans. An on-air caller with a question. Blip—ten minutes. Over. Done. What? What just happened? Where am I? How did I get here?

Just like that. Ten minutes, 22,080 units, over $400,000 in sales—seemingly unfathomable: $44,116 per *minute*.

Host: "Nick, thanks for bringing your product to us today. . . ."

Huh? Screech. Halt. Snap back to reality.

Let me put that in slow motion. Forty—four—thousand—one—hundred—sixteen—dollars—per miiiiinnnnnnuuuuute. This is *not* the part of the story where the writer interjects, "and then he woke up." It's the part of the story where I come forward and say, "That's what happened to me." This is my story. What happened to me is what happens to many others just like me every day at QVC. Everyday people with a new or existing product, broadcast into the homes of millions of people, are generating millions of dollars in sales.

The possibility of this happening once you're lucky enough to step on the set at QVC in the small Philadelphia suburb of West Chester, Pennsylvania, all comes down to numbers. Millions of people watching, a small percentage of them dialing in to buy, and you're on your way to selling thousands upon thousands of units in virtually no time at all.

QVC—the largest home shopping channel, whose name stands for *quality, value, convenience*—is the power of leverage at work, and leverage is the vital component of any product and business success story. If you're reading this book and you have a product already developed or you're thinking of one, you've undoubtedly walked this problematic path before. How do you maximize your marketing efforts using as little human and fiscal resources as possible?

Whether you are an entrepreneur, small business, and even an established business with a substantial budget, your success is contingent on making smart marketing decisions that go a long way for as low a cost as possible.

When I first came to QVC, I did just about everything for my business. I created the products, I researched and contracted for the material involved in production, wrote the directions that went into the kit, created the Web site to support the product, researched trade shows for exhibiting, built the trade show displays, made the product samples—the list goes on and on, but it begins and ends with smart marketing.

I estimate the amount of time I spent marketing my products out of my then 70- to 80-hour work weeks was—sadly, but all too realistically—about 6 hours a week. If you're doing just about everything in your own business like I was, you know what I'm talking about. For others, trust that what I'm saying is true. It's a sad fact facing most entrepreneurs and small businesses in the beginning of the growth stage.

The tighter your budget or timeline, the more important it is to make connections with companies that can allow you to maximize your efforts using as little resources as possible. It's critical for profits and growth, and it's important for penetrating the market quickly. By finding QVC, I gained a massive lever under arguably the largest obstacle facing any new product—marketing. With this one connection I essentially gained a workforce numbering in the thousands—people taking phone calls, fulfilling product, operating cameras, marketing—all supporting my product during any given on-air stint.

But what is even more remarkable about my experience on that particular day is that I was selling a niche product. *A niche product* is something that is manufactured and marketed for specialized uses. By its very nature, it only appeals to a small part of a given market.

The fact that I sold over $400,000 of a niche product is hard to believe for many, given that when you tune in to QVC—or any other home shopping show or infomercial, for that matter—what you usually see are products that fit into the very description of mass appeal. These are items like jewelry, fitness equipment, weight-loss products, or fancy kitchen gizmos—things that attract large numbers of people because they are used by many people and have a place in every home. A large market plus large appeal add up to a greater chance of success.

But in my case, the phenomenal numbers QVC and I put up on the board that day (and for many appearances thereafter) came not from a mass-market product, but from a plastic template system that shows how to make your own gift bag out of any kind of paper, called the Kreate-a-bag®.

Now, you might be seeing a big red flashing sign in your mind inscribed with the simple question, *"What?"* But that is exactly my point. My product appeals to only a small part of a medium-sized industry—crafts. However, I was showing it to millions of eager people at the same time on the largest home shopping channel in the world. It might not have been a piece of exercise equipment, but I exercised leverage in a big way that day!

At the same time, it's important to understand that not every item on QVC is a runaway success because of the massive exposure. You do have to have a great product, and the Kreate-a-bag® was and still is just that. This is not a shameless plug, but the Kreate-a-bag® is not only the first template system that shows anyone how to make their own gift bag, it's also easy and fast. Plus, it has the vital component of emotion built into it because it provides gratification to the users when they custom-make a gift bag as part of their gift to a loved one.

Additionally, it saves people money. At the time of this particular big day on QVC, a single gift bag cost about $5. So, by allowing an individual to make their own, they only had to make four bags to pay for the $20 kit. The point is this: Although the massive exposure is critical, it's not the only reason behind your product's success. Demand and innovation play a vital role as well along with a host of other variables. (If you are curious about the Kreate-a-bag® you can view a short video of how it works at www.GreenSneakers.com/giftbag).

There are only a handful of places where a small or large business can sell 22,080 units in such a short period of time, and QVC is on the top of the list. In addition to the exposure and the benefits of your product, however, there are many other elements that lead to success.

When you are on-air, it's like having your product next to the cash register at your local superstore, and two million people are standing there at the same time looking at it, thinking about putting it into their cart as they check out.

The big difference is that the person working the cash register is a trusted friend that you see all the time, and your friend is demonstrating the item to you while the other two million people look over your shoulder. After five minutes, you've all seen how it works and what it can do for you.

But wait, there's more. In the middle of the demonstration, someone in the line behind you shouts, "I bought one, and it's awesome. In fact, I'm here to buy another one." Short of being able to touch it, now you're confident that it's what you've been wanting all along, and it is at your fingertips. You make your move and take it home with you.

The Kreate-a-bag® was not the first product that I sold on QVC. It was my second. I had been successfully selling my first product, the envelope template that I mentioned in the introduction, for a couple of years. Then, one day, my buyer asked, "So, what else do you have?"

I thought to myself, what more do I need?

"Bring us something else related to the envelope maker," she said.

Now, I hadn't really given much thought to expanding. Back then I thought I was going to be a one-hit wonder. I was proud of it, and I was taking the ride for all it was worth. After all, I didn't know anything about crafts. I was a jock in high school. I liked to be outdoors. I didn't know anything about retail, and I didn't want to learn. The Kreate-a-lope® was it for me and was all there ever would be for me. It was a goldmine. I was going to make millions of dollars with it, then retire to live a life of leisure. These were my thoughts. Foolish, short-sighted young man I was at the time.

When the buyer asked me for a complementary product, I realized I had nothing to lose. I wasn't doing anything else. So, I went home and started toiling, and I came up with my second item. My agent and I made the presentation a short time later, and much to my surprise, the buyer turned to me and said, "Let's do a key launch."

"Uh, okay," I responded. She looked at me like I knew what I was doing, like I knew the rules of the game at QVC. Whatever she said, it sounded good to me. They use a lot of terms like this at QVC to signify big things. I looked at my agent and said, "I'm in, but what's a key launch?"

In short, a key launch back then was a bigger-than-usual introduction of a new product that would get promoted in advance of its on-air debut. The item would also get promoted heavily on the day of the appearance, and, if needed, would air as many as four times in one day.

Today, QVC still does key launches but they're generally scheduled for two appearances. And there are other promotions that include host promos, power promos, one-time offers, and the big everyday promo—the most coveted of all—the TSV. *TSV* stands for today's special value. QVC begins selling the TSV at midnight and continues selling it throughout the day in as many as 12 spots. At the writing of this book, TSVs are expected to sell a minimum of $1,400,000 in one day with many being prepped for numbers as high as $2,500,000.

CHAPTER

2

The Home Shopping Phenomenon

Before I get into how it was possible to generate nearly half a million dollars in ten minutes, let's back up and take a look at the abbreviated history of the home shopping phenomenon and bring it to the present in order to understand the opportunities available moving forward.

Mail-order Catalogs

The home shopping industry has roots dating all the way back to 1744, when Ben Franklin created what is believed to be the first mail-order catalog in the United States. It featured scientific and academic books and bore the promise, "Those persons who live remote, by sending their orders and money to B. Franklin, may depend on the same justice as if present."

Over a century later in 1872, Aaron Montgomery Ward published the first catalog for his Montgomery Ward mail-order business and within two decades grew his original single-sheet catalog to one consisting of more than 500 pages selling more than 20,000 items. Many others soon followed.

Commercials and Infomercials

The 1940s saw the inception of the television commercial. For the first time in history, consumers could see a product explained and demonstrated to them without chancing upon a traveling peddler. It was better than paging through a catalog—viewers could see the product in three dimensions and watch how it worked! Early pioneers of this new style of product marketing included Ron Popeil, who popularized the medium with products such as the Chop-O-Matic.

During the 1950s and 1960s, the Federal Communications Commission (FCC) created regulations that limited commercial airtime to twelve minutes per hour. But in 1984, the FCC changed its regulations governing the limit of advertising on television, and the infomercial proliferated. Cable television stations had many low-cost slots available for product producers, and consumers could easily pick up a phone, call a toll-free number, and use their credit card to make a purchase.

Today, the infomercial is a staple of our society. Many large and small companies alike are making a mark and creating millions of dollars in sales for themselves. They're creating brand recognition, and once-no-name individuals are becoming household names. But still, for many, the entry cost and risk are too high to enter this billion-dollar industry.

Home Shopping Channels

In 1977, a local radio station in Clearwater, Florida, was facing cash-flow problems. One of its delinquent advertisers, a local appliance store, was also having financial challenges. In lieu of cash, station manager Lowell "Bud" Paxson was offered payment in the form of 112 can openers!

He returned to the station with his bounty and instructed the on-air host, Bob Circosta, to sell the can openers after one of the regular news segments. The can openers were pitched for $9.95 each, and customers had to come to the radio station to pick them up. They sold every one of them, and an industry was born.

In 1982, Paxson and a man named Roy Speer launched the Home Shopping Club. In 1985, the station went national under the name it is recognized by today, HSN, which stands for the Home Shopping Network.

The meteoric rise and success of HSN was soon followed by QVC, which stands for quality, value, convenience. By no small irony, QVC was founded by Joseph Segel, the founder of the Franklin Mint, whose namesake is credited with creating the first mail-order catalog in the United States, mentioned at the opening of this chapter.

Today, QVC is the undisputed champion of the home shopping industry. In 2005 its worldwide sales topped $6.5 billion and its U.S. viewership reached 87 million. HSN's worldwide sales for the same period tallied $3.05 billion, while maintaining a U.S. audience of 89 million homes. QVC is ranked the second largest television network in the United States after CBS, as reported by Broadcasting & Cable in 2005.

Golden Opportunities

The essence of QVC and HSN is that they are the core of catalog shopping for the visual generation. They offer the simple convenience of demonstrating products to those interested in watching from the comfort of their own home.

With 24-hour-a-day programming these stations reach rural buyers, insomniacs, shift workers, home-bound consumers, people looking to avoid a crowd, or those interested in fast and easy shopping. They reach just about anybody with a television and have products for sale in just about any category, and more than you'll find in most major stores. The stations can also be watched online via a home computer with an Internet connection.

Home shopping is big business, and never before in its history has it been this accessible for small and large businesses alike. In the following chapters you will see the true power of QVC and the speed at which one can enter a marketplace. You will learn how to find new ideas and develop existing ones, how QVC can be a springboard for other mediums of sales and distribution, and how to get on and stay on QVC for the long haul.

CHAPTER

3

How to Find or Create
Hot Products

If Necessity is the mother of Invention, then Laziness is her step-sister. You need to look no further than your own home to see great innovations that are a response to these two close relatives.

To my older brother, I was the solution to a big problem in our house. I solved both necessity and supported his laziness. What I'm referring to is a typical day in our house growing up that involved watching television.

Before the convenience of remote controls and cable television, I would repeatedly be commanded by my imposing brother to change the channel, often having to sit by the TV until he decided what he wanted to watch. Should the station suddenly lose reception—because cable had not yet come into mainstream existence—I would don the hat of signal modulator and jockey the rabbit ears of our television in hopes that it would quickly clear up the signal. Even several years later, when we installed an aerial antenna on our roof that was controlled from within the house, I was the one responsible for manning the controls at the behest of my threatening brother.

Now, had my brother delved into the family tree of Invention, he would not only have found Necessity as the mother, and Laziness as the stepsister, but he would have found the cousin of Invention who goes by the name of Motivation. Had my brother been motivated, or I for that matter, we could have pioneered the solution to the problem undoubtedly plaguing many TV watchers in the world—how to change the station without getting up, and how to get better reception.

Taking a lesson from the experience of my youth, there are three simple questions to ask in order to begin on the path to creating or finding your own hot products:

1. How can I solve the problem?
2. How can I make life easier?
3. How can I make something better?

These three questions and the discipline to brainstorm or seek out answers are vital to developing great solutions.

Improve an Existing Product

Take an existing product and look for areas of opportunity. An area of opportunity can be defined as any aspect of the product that is lacking in any way. This could be-faults in the design, construction, how it works, how it is used, and so on. The list can be exhaustive—and should be.

To help you do this, apply the three aforementioned questions (including derivatives) to the product exploring every possible avenue. For example, you can ask: How can I solve the problem better than the current design does? How can I make the product better? Is it too expensive? Can I make it cheaper? Can I change the color and make it look more appealing? Can I make it easier to use? Keep at it until you've torn the product apart in every possible area.

When you are finished, you should be able to identify any area that is lacking that can be exploited and improved upon with new technology, redesign, and more. In many cases, the end result could be an entirely new concept, a patentable idea perhaps, or simply an improvement that can make the item more appealing. One example of how this technique was applied to great success is the case of the everyday household fan. Fans have been around for a long time. They have been created to fit windows, ceilings, or to be placed on counters. Some have tall stands and some swivel. Not much innovation there since its inception—that is, until 1989.

In the 1940s and 1950s, the O.A. Sutton Company out of Wichita, Kansas, built the original Vornado fans. Constructed out of turned-aluminum, the innovative fans performed superbly and were well received by the public. In the 1950s, according to the company's Web site, one out of every three fans sold in the United States was a Vornado fan.

Then in 1989, a new company was formed. Engineers found that by applying vortex action technology to a household fan, air could be moved greater distances—a simple response to the question, How can we make it better? They modified the traditional cage or mesh cover of the fan with a spiral ribbed cover. They found that by simulating the air in the funnel of a tornado, unparalleled air circulation could be created. Voila! A new patent was issued in 1992, and a new line of fans was introduced, revitalizing a staid industry and capitalizing on the brand name created years prior.

The Vornado fan is just one of many new products in our society emerging from old solutions to problems and challenges that still exist. The foundations for ideas like this can be found everywhere in great abundance. One easy place to find a product that might be improved upon is the United States Patent Office. Oftentimes, patents are filed on viable products but that for some reason never reach the marketplace. Others, like the Vornado fan, reach the marketplace with great success and then lose steam. With the power of the Internet, it has never been easier to research old patents to find possible opportunities for new products. A simple search on www.google.com/patents can have your brain turning in a vortex of existing and old products, finding areas of opportunity for years to come.

Research

If you have no idea what to sell, even if you have a product that you've already been working on, it's time to get acquainted with Invention's long lost son, Research.

Internet

With the advent of the Internet, what used to take weeks can now be done in a few hours. Trends and demand can help you ascertain the feasibility of your idea and market potential, and there is no shortage of free and paid services available to do this vital information reconnaissance.

The Internet literally measures the move of every surfer, and much of the information is mined. Those that know where and what to look for can benefit greatly by finding out what is hot and on the edge of booming before spending another precious moment guessing and, in many cases, plunging forward ignorantly.

For anyone with an idea already formulated, or on the edge of being initiated, this research can substantiate any further investment of time and money, or stop you dead in your tracks if the results are less than promising. Because of the ever-changing location of various online tools, I've listed a few resources in the back of the book, with a complete list available under Free Resources at www.SellonQ.com.

Simple online searches combining key terms can help you find hot trends. For example, searching for "eBay what's hot" will produce results that will lead you to eBay's Seller Central page, where you will have the ability to view reports on what's hot by category, see historical market research, and more. And since eBay is a sizeable barometer of consumer interests, the marketplace tendencies you discover can be a great asset when used to help formulate an idea or expand an existing one.

Another great way to use the Internet for research is by finding forums in your category of interest and reading the posts. It has been speculated that writers of a recently popular television series peruse the forums looking for new ideas. Whether the resulting episodes actually mimicked the theories of various forum users is debatable, the fact remains that people will post problems and questions online that might lead to your next great idea.

Trade Shows

The result of research often ends up in the form of new products that are being exhibited at industry trade fairs. This is not intended as a shortcut by any means, but trade shows are a viable way to find new and exciting trends that are emerging in the marketplace. They can also help you spot problems that people have attempted to solve. If you are thinking of a product or have one already, being aware of what is and has been in existence is very important. Plus, if you have a knack for inventing, it is likely you will be able to spot something in need of improvement.

If you attend a trade show, look for a new product showcase. This is a common feature found at most venues created by show promoters to assist companies in presenting their latest and greatest products. Additionally, many trade shows have an area of the exhibition dedicated solely to new vendors. These are often very exciting places to be because the innovative heart of idea people can be found there. As a marketing person, agent, or someone interested in finding great products or spotting trends, these represent target-rich environments. Crowds will gather around innovation, and a buzz can be seen, felt, and heard. Of course, this is not to say that innovation can't be found elsewhere in any given trade show.

Overseas trade fairs are also a viable place to find and spot new trends. People living in different cultures and environments think differently but have many of the same needs and problems as many in our part of the world have. Their way of thinking can lead them to solving problems differently than their American counterparts, and so many fresh ideas might be found that can nurture your insights. Again, like stateside trade shows, these too, can be a great feeding ground for a marketing person or agent looking to establish a relationship with a manufacturer or inventor interested in introducing their product to new markets.

Great ideas don't come from stale thought patterns. They come from active and curious minds that see and experience new things. Open-minded wandering and exploration can lead to discovery. In my own experience, I've often come up with a great idea by misinterpreting someone else's idea. Meaning, I have often thought a given invention was solving one problem when, in actuality, it solved another. I call this accidental inventing.

Accidental inventing also often happens when people set out to accomplish one thing but arrive at something different in the process. Post-it Notes, the sticky-enough-but-not-too-sticky paper pads that are used for posting reminders in office and home environments, is an example of this phenomenon.

The glue used in Post-It Notes was originally intended to be a strong adhesive. Later, it was applied to hold bookmarkers in place by a colleague of the inventor, and an entirely new purpose for the glue was born.

Being in the gap between what you think something is and what it actually is, is the same as brainstorming for solutions with no tethers. It is the place where you can listen to your inner impulses. This is where I believe Creativity, the father of Invention, resides. It is in this place where inspiration works in a flash and I find fertile grounds for this free-thinking when walking a trade show floor with an open, "loose" mind.

Magazines and Books

Publications such as magazines, trade journals, and books on your area of interest can also provide the juxtaposition that allows creativity to come into play, as well as being able to foster the other seeds of inspiration mentioned earlier.

It has been said that many an accomplished writer has penned an original story unknowingly in the essence of works by authors they have come to be inspired by—as if by osmosis. The mere exposure to something can work on conscious and unconscious levels, playing a part in new and original concepts in areas of writing, much like reading and researching magazines and books about the subject of your own interests can have an influence on your own new and original product creations.

It is important to crunch data and digest trends, but only as a means to becoming open to your inner voice of inspiration and creativity. Although many may misinterpret the ideas of this chapter as being about getting ideas from others, I urge you to see the collective process of being inspired and finding your own solutions to problems that readily exist, not merely copying the hard work of others. The world is full of ideas, and the opportunities for finding solutions are endless. In that light, I end this chapter by repeating the three questions that can help you nurture new and exciting products from which the world can benefit:

1. How can I solve the problem?
2. How can I make life easier?
3. How can I make something better?

CHAPTER 4

Be First and Fastest to Mass Market

I f you take a close look at the traditional options available for selling your product to the masses, you will quickly find that the process is generally not a short one. It is a process that is both costly in the currency of time and of financial resources.

QVC, by contrast, offers one of the best ways to be first and fastest to the marketplace that, by its very nature, is also one of the most inexpensive avenues for reaching the mass market with your product.

Generally, when you have a product that you want to introduce and sell to the public, you have two ways to accomplish your goal. You can sell directly to retailers or directly to consumers. Within these two paths, there are endless possibilities, but this chapter will provide an overview of two top choices, then compare them to QVC. The first is selling directly to stores with physical locations and the second is selling directly to consumers via infomercials.

Selling to Stores: Overview

In retail, past and present, the evolution of product development begins with a new idea. You either stumble into it, if you're like me, or you are an existing company constantly developing new ideas that will meet your customer needs.

Once you determine that there is a demand for the item, a typical next step involves testing the product, developing the product's contents, directions, and packaging, making decisions on pricing, and so on. At the very least, if you want to sell to stores you'll need a prototype, so you strive to create a working model of the contents and packaging. The steps up to this point are a considerable investment of time, energy, and financial resources.

Once you have your product ready for the market, you have to sell it. You can make appointments with store owners, do mailers, advertise in magazines, or participate in trade shows. Again, a lot of time, money, and energy are spent bringing your product to market—all before you have a single sale.

Now, if you're an established business and your new product is in the same industry and channels you have already established, it's a lot easier to add it to your product pipeline and have buyers you already know give you a purchase order. But generally speaking, even this is often challenging.

Next, the time factor comes into play. How long will it take before you know whether your product will be successful? In retail, once you go through the entire process of developing, packaging, manufacturing, and getting your product into stores, you have to wait about twelve months before you know if you have a success on your hands. Add this to the six months you already spent developing your idea. If your product does not do well, you have lost not only the eighteen months, but the financial resources you spent taking this avenue.

QVC versus Selling to Stores

Keep in mind that I'm not saying that going direct to stores is by any means a negative choice. In fact, it should be a comprehensive part of your approach. But for understanding the strengths of QVC in regard to being first and fastest to the marketplace along with cost effectiveness, it is imperative to compare it to marketing a new product to stores in a mutually exclusive manner.

So what makes marketing a new product on QVC, in most cases, better than marketing the same product directly to stores?

For the most part, it's more cost effective to market via QVC. When my company does consumer trade shows, it takes *four* events, in four different cities, with a team of people working eight hours a day, Friday, Saturday, and Sunday, plus the travel time, to make the same profit we can make in one six-minute spot on QVC. Similarly, industry trade shows, where we are selling direct to retailers, also offer less-than-stellar returns on our investment of time and money. Again, as stated earlier, I do believe trade shows should be part of most companies' marketing plans, as they have been ours, but when compared on a one-to-one basis for immediate impact, QVC is consistently the more effective choice.

Another reason QVC stands above selling to stores when it comes to launching or selling a new product is because developing a product to sell on QVC involves less time and money spent on packaging. With QVC, the item is being shipped directly to the consumer from a QVC warehouse and does not require colorful graphics for in-store display. This eliminates expense in design and production.

There are also no costs involved in producing the traditional marketing tools used in promoting products to stores. This includes, sell sheets, catalogs, building or purchasing trade show booths, and participating in promotional advertising.

Lastly, selling a product on QVC provides immediate results. You know in less than ten minutes how your product has been received, as opposed to the traditionally lengthy time it takes to measure results when selling in stores.

A side-by-side comparison of selling to stores versus QVC produces the following summary of pros and cons:

	Selling to Stores	QVC
Time to market	6–18 months	3–5 months
Determining whether you have a successful product	6–12 months	immediate results
Graphical packaging	required	not necessary
Creating brochures for marketing	highly recommended	not necessary
Exhibiting at trade shows	highly recommended	not necessary
Creating trade show booth	highly recommended	not necessary
Mailing brochures	highly recommended	not necessary
Advertising	highly recommended	not necessary

Infomercials—Direct to Consumers: Overview

In the days of black-and-white television, Ron Popeil, known for the Pocket Fisherman, the Vegamatic, and, in recent times, the Food Dehydrator and the Rotisserie Oven, among other things, was one of the first to perfect the use of television to sell products directly to consumers.

Many of the techniques he implemented are still in use today, like the bonus offer: "And if you call now, you'll get the super deluxe self-cleaning widget for free!"

The Ronco Spray Gun

***Ron Popeil's first television commercial (circa 1950s), from* The Salesman of the Century**

While still demonstrating products at Woolworth's in Chicago, I began my first entry into the TV marketing business. It all began because I wanted to take advantage of the new medium of television. A friend told me about a TV station in Tampa, Florida, where you could make commercials for $550. Another pal told me about a new garden accessory that could wash your car and fertilize your lawn, and that sounded to me like a perfect TV product.

We went to the Chicago-based manufacturer, and I bought a small quantity, which eventually grew to several hundred thousand pieces. I named it the Ronco Spray Gun and began advertising them on TV, in Springfield and Rockford, Illinois, and Madison, Wisconsin.

We eventually went national and sold nearly 1 million Spray Guns in four years.

Taken from *The Salesman of the Century* by Ron Popeil and Jefferson Graham. 1995, Delacorte Press: page 45.

We've come to know this longer style of advertising as an infomercial, and it predates QVC by several decades. Like QVC, it shares some of the same benefits over selling to stores, one being the speed in which you know whether you have a successful product in your midst. Yes, you still have to spend time developing your product and manufacturing it. Yes, you have to spend time creating the infomercial. But where you don't spend time is in finding out if your product will be successful. When your infomercial airs, the phones either ring or they don't.

Additionally, infomercials share with QVC the same benefit of lower expenditures of time and money for product development when compared to selling to stores. Again, this is because shipping direct to the consumer alleviates the cost of developing colorful packaging and the additional cost it takes to manufacture this kind of packaging. The expense of bringing your product to market, however, differs when compared to selling to stores, in that it does not involve traveling to trade shows and to the locations of buyers. Instead, bringing your product to market via the infomercial route involves the expense of creating an infomercial and then purchasing media time for on-air broadcasting.

Although discussing infomercials in depth is beyond the scope of this book, it is essential to explain how they function and the approximate costs involved in order to understand why QVC is a top choice for new and established businesses to bring their products to market.

Costs involved to produce a basic infomercial are about $100,000 and higher. Once the infomercial is created, you then have to find a place to broadcast it—more money. The cost of purchasing media time varies greatly, depending on local, regional, or national coverage, and is also based on time of day, the size of the viewing audience, the length of your infomercial, and so on.

Add in the fact that media rates are climbing because, as the infomercial industry grows (currently estimated to be in the neighborhood of $90 billion), stations have been raising their rates to capture part of this success. Moreover, rising costs are a normal occurrence in any industry.

Needless to say, the costs of going the infomercial route add up quickly.

QVC versus an Infomercial

Keep in mind in this section that the arguments serve to make a comparison, not a case against using this strategy for marketing your products. I do believe infomercials should be used in conjunction with QVC when appropriate, much like selling to stores is an essential part of most comprehensive product marketing strategies.

If QVC has advantages over selling direct to stores, what sets it apart from an infomercial? The answer lies in the relationship between QVC and you, its vendor.

When you go on QVC, you do not pay for airtime and you do not pay for production. QVC is live 364 days of the year. It does not broadcast on Christmas and it does not tape any airings. What you see is what you see, with no delay. And this translates to hundreds of thousands of dollars in savings for you.

Remember when I said it costs at least $100,000 to film an infomercial and then you have to pay for the airtime to broadcast it? This is one of the major differences between having your product on QVC and creating and broadcasting an infomercial. By marketing your product on QVC, you don't have to outlay this otherwise upfront cost.

Speaking of money, one can make an argument that selling your product via an infomercial is more profitable than selling on QVC because in an infomercial the product is something that is sold by you, the manufacturer, directly to the consumer and the money flows directly to you. Whereas, when you sell on QVC you are splitting profits.

Although any given situation varies and would need to be examined on a case-by-case basis, generally speaking, when you sell via an infomercial you have to shoulder most of the expenses that QVC absorbs. These include the cost of airtime, the cost of the phone bank that takes and processes the orders, credit card fees, product fulfillment, warehousing, and so on.

What these costs are and how they affect your profit margin depends on any number of variables, but the point is, what might seem to be an obvious advantage for selling via an infomercial (getting the full profit) soon begins to dissipate upon closer inspection, often showing itself to be a large disadvantage.

Another advantage of working with QVC is that when you present your product to QVC, you begin a collaborative effort. If your product does not show promise, QVC won't waste anyone's time and money just to put your product on-air.

QVC wants success just as much as you do. It relies on past data and experience and current trends to make decisions. According to QVC's Web site, its high-tech data center stores as much as 19 terabytes of data. To put it in perspective, it would take 50,000 trees to produce enough paper to print a terabyte of data, and it would take a forest of 750,000 trees to hold what the data center stores. So, needless to say, QVC sees thousands of products every day, and it has years and years of hard numbers to rely on.

Additionally, the buyers and planners bring a human element to the forefront. They have their own experience and insights to call on in order to arrive at the most risk-averse conclusion for them and your product.

Further, if you are represented by an agent, it is likely that the agent has years of experience and hard numbers to rely on as well. Agents also have to make intelligent decisions in order to survive, in that they are only as successful as the products they elect to represent. Their skills are sharpened further by being limited to the number of products they can physically find and present to QVC. So, by having an agent on your team you have another trusted mind to help you move forward. Chapter 6 covers agents in more depth.

If your product is not successful on QVC, people are held accountable and jobs can be lost. For this reason, the people at QVC strive to be correct in their assumptions, and they'll tell you what they think of your product in order to increase its chances of being a hit. This might come in the form of a suggested improvement or a recommended change in configuration. They also might suggest incorporating the product into a successful segment with an already proven marquee personality, such as someone famous in your industry. This level of endorsement might be just what your product needs to be a winner.

By contrast, infomercials don't generally come with a group of "consultants" of this magnitude. If you want to create an infomercial, there are plenty of production companies willing to take your money to create an infomercial segment for you. Whether your infomercial is successful is where the line of responsibility ends, in most cases. As I said in the opening of this chapter, infomercials should be considered as part of a comprehensive strategy when appropriate. Many products on QVC have run concurrent to infomercials produced after and before the product was a hit on QVC. That said, a side-by-side comparison of infomercials versus QVC produces the following summary of pros and cons:

	Infomercial	QVC
Cost of producing segment	your cost	no direct cost to you
Cost of airtime	your cost	no direct cost to you
Cost of taking phone calls	your cost	no direct cost to you
Cost of processing credit cards	your cost	no direct cost to you
Cost of warehousing	your cost	no direct cost to you
Decision to broadcast	solitary effort	collaborative decision
Sales/profit	full amt of sale to you	split the amount of sale
Media placement	media placement varies	usually targeted by category

Summary

QVC can be a vital part to launching a new or existing product from both a monetary and marketing perspective. Although I compared three popular avenues for marketing a product to the masses in a mutually exclusive way, I believe that integrating all three, along with many of the other options available, is the best way to capture a market share for your product and reap maximum profits.

In my journey, I didn't have the experience or the financial resources to consider many other choices for my new product, and QVC was the perfect fit. It allowed my company to launch many new products and slowly integrate them into other methods of distribution by generating the capital to grow our business. Looking back in hindsight, if I only had one choice for marketing my product and wanted to be first and fastest to the market with minimum investment of time and money, I would still choose QVC.

CHAPTER 5

How to Protect Your Product

believe the best way to make your mark is by being first and fastest to the market in a comprehensive manner, especially if you can readily make your product identifiable with an unforgettable name. In addition to this ideal situation, taking advantage of any and all methods of protecting your product is a critical step to gaining a market advantage.

Patents

When it comes to taking steps to legally protect your product however, first and foremost, a plethora of information has been authored by experts on the topic of patenting and protecting your inventions and products. I encourage you to read it, and a good place to start is the United States Patent and Trademark Office. Its main Web site is www.uspto.gov and the online resource center for inventors is www.uspto.gov/web/offices/com/iip/index.htm.

This chapter does not contain authoritative legal advice but, rather, provides an overview of things I've come to learn and experience. As in all things of legal nature, I encourage you to find a competent attorney.

I do believe in patents immensely, despite the arguments that many can be side-stepped, and they are often expensive. I encourage anyone to file for one if the opportunity presents itself because, not only are patents useful as a layer of protection, but they are also a saleable commodity that can provide great value should you decide that selling or licensing your intellectual property is in your best interest. The cost of obtaining a patent varies greatly, depending on any number of variables such as the type and complexity of the application, and the time it takes to obtain one can sometimes take years.

Whether you decide to file for a patent or not, you should take copious notes as you develop your idea. This includes the date you came up with the idea, drawings you've created with dates, changes to drawings with dates, and any information that can be used to substantiate the evolution of your product.

Another important step is to conduct a patent search. A patent search involves researching existing and pending applications related to your idea. If you find a patent that matches your invention exactly, you will save a considerable expense by not filing a similar application and also, by not moving forward unknowingly and infringing on an existing patent.

There are many competent patent search professionals you can use to conduct such a search and most will sign a non-disclosure agreement well in advance of asking you to share your idea with them. Keep in mind that once you share your idea with someone else—this includes attempting to sell or license your idea—you only have one year in the United States to apply for a patent. Again, consult with an attorney to understand your full rights.

With regard to overseas protection, if you go public with your idea, you forgo your ability to file for overseas protection unless you have already filed for a U.S. patent. And U.S. patents only protect items in the United States.

Invention Submission Companies

Invention submission companies is a hot topic among product creators. The typical invention submission company offers an assessment of your idea/invention and promises to market your product to companies on your behalf for a substantial fee. The problem is, there are a lot of scavengers preying on inventors. This is not to say that every invention submission company or firm specializing in assisting inventors in areas of marketing is a scam, but there have been, and continue to be, many that take advantage of people hoping to market their product. For this reason, due diligence is essential on your part if you are considering using a third party for any services involving your product or idea. The official Web site of the Federal Trade Commission (FTC), www.ftc.com, is one place among many online that has information about unscrupulous firms.

I have never used an invention submission company, but I have heard both positive and negative reports from those who have: Simply beware.

Many inventors and product developers choose to license their ideas or products to large companies. When you enter into a typical licensing arrangement you grant the rights to your idea/product to an individual, company, or other entity, in return for a fee. The fee can be a straight royalty against sales, a flat fee upfront, or any combination of these or other exchanges deemed to be of value.

Licensing your idea/product serves several purposes. First, a well-selected company should have the financial resources to market your idea/product to its maximum potential. Second, a suitable company should have the ability to protect your intellectual property from the infringements of others.

Although the focus of this chapter is on protecting your product, I'll digress here for a moment to provide an overview of how licensing can impact your bottom line.

One of the benefits of licensing your product is that you don't have to do the work of marketing or manufacturing. If you've selected a good company to handle your product for you, sales should be much higher than what you could have done yourself. Plus, you won't have any expenses. The downside to all of this however, is that you will only be receiving a royalty and not your normal profit margin.

On the other hand, if you decide to go it alone and can get on QVC with your product, you might be able to realize substantial profits, and doors to stores and distributors might be opened as a result of the exposure you gain from being on TV.

That said, thinking through the licensing possibility should be a thorough process. Consider this example: You build a product for a cost of $5, sell it to QVC for $10, and QVC, in turn, sells it on-air for $20. Your approximate profit would be $5 per unit. Take that times 4,000 units, and your profit, if you sell every unit in stock, would be

$20,000. Conversely, if you licensed the item to a company for an industry average of 5 percent based on the wholesale cost, in this example $10, then your per-unit royalties would be $0.50, and in the same example of selling 4,000 units would yield $2,000.

Now, you might think, who in their right mind would license their products when they can make so much more doing it themselves? The short argument is that licensing your product can gain you greater distribution across the board, at no effort on your part. You might be able to make hundreds of thousands of dollars, even millions, without lifting a finger beyond your initial efforts. If you can find and create a licensing arrangement, you should compare it to having to take all the financial risk, arranging participation in trade shows, and spending money on other promotions with no guarantee of a profit, and so on. There is a lot to be said about licensing. I don't recommend taking it lightly.

The QVC avenue is not to be tossed aside easily either. In the best of both worlds, you might be able to enter into an agreement that affords you the rights to handle QVC by yourself while licensing your store sales to other, more capable companies. And in light of protecting your product, by being first to market via QVC, you can gain a market edge and/or brand name recognition that will deter your competitors or knockoffs.

For more information about licensing visit, www.SellonQ.com and click on Free Resources.

Trademarks

As I mentioned in the opening of this chapter, consider the strength of your brand name and the protection it can afford.

When you hear the term *Band-aid,* you think of the thing you place on your cuts. Everybody knows what one is. All priorities considered, after you fall down and cry for your mommy, you yell for a Band-aid. But what does the competition call their products? They can't call them Band-aids because Band-aid is a registered trademark. They have to describe it as what it is—an adhesive gauze pad with a sticky strip attached. When you're laying on the pavement in agony, it's a real mouthful to scream out, "I need an adhesive gauze pad with a sticky strip attached!" It's not much of a visual picture from a marketing perspective, either, since we've all already indelibly labeled that adhesive strip with the gauze pad as a Band-aid.

The same reality holds true for Disney characters, Cabbage Patch dolls, Barney, Coca-Cola, Apple computers, and countless others, including my own niche of envelope templates registered with the trademark office as Kreate-a-lope®.

Having a registered trademark can be significantly cheaper than acquiring a patent and yet might offer you a considerable amount of protection, especially when combined with a patent. General practice to protect a name is to use the letters TM in association with the phrase you hope to protect. Once you file for a trademark and it gets registered, the TM can be replaced by®. Again, consult with an attorney when in doubt.

Copyrights

Copyrights can also be used to protect a product. You can copyright forms of expression like books, songs, directions, computer programs, movies, photographs, and many others. A general rule of thumb is to include this symbol with each body of work: ©.

Trade Secrets

Another form of protection you may be able to utilize is to keep the ingredients of your product a secret, if there are any secret formulations. You can also keep your manufacturing process a secret if it is unique.

With regards to the former, you might have developed a fire-retardant chemical concoction that can make all materials flame resistant. Filing for a patent would divulge its ingredients. The same holds true for cosmetics that might remove wrinkles. And then there is Kentucky Fried Chicken. Although I'm not sure the recipe could be patented, it sure could have been copyrighted. However, it was not, to the best of my knowledge, and the secret recipe remains in a vault, known to few. The same is true with Coca-Cola.

Regarding the latter, your manufacturing process might involve a certain method for applying materials. You might have to formulate your dolls in 101 degree heat in order to get the proper texture on their skin. By keeping this a secret you are in essence protecting your product.

Nondisclosure Forms

If your invention is determined to be unpatentable, the best way to protect yourself is to have interested parties sign a nondisclosure agreement, also called a confidentiality agreement. If someone uses your secret after signing a nondisclosure agreement, you can sue for damages. The Internet contains many free forms that you can download for examples of what you might need when consulting an attorney for this important form.

Provisional Application for Patent

Since June 8, 1995, the United States Patent and Trademark Office (USPTO) has offered inventors the option of filing a provisional application for patent, which was designed to provide a lower-cost first patent filing in the United States. Filing this application is a low-cost way of obtaining patent-pending status, which serves as a deterrent if you intend on showing your invention to others. Visit www.uspto.gov for more details.

Liability Insurance

Suffer a lawsuit, and you might lose your livelihood. It's a sad fact in our litigious society. To protect yourself, the vehicle most commonly used is liability insurance. QVC requires it, and so do many retail stores. Finding an insurance provider is a simple task that can be handled in a few minutes with a phone book or the Internet. As of this writing, QVC requires $1,000,000 worth of coverage, which translates to a fairly inexpensive premium. It protects you as well, so it should not be overlooked.

Believe in the power of positive thinking, and let's hope you are a runaway success protected along your journey in all ways.

6

How to Get on QVC

I t has been said that it is harder to get on QVC than it is to get in a movie with Al Pacino or Robert DeNiro. In August 2003, South Jersey's *Courier Post* newspaper reported 1,600 hopeful vendors from all over the country went to QVC headquarters for a single open-call product tryout. During the entire previous year, according to the Wall Street Journal Online, 13,000 inquiries were received from would-be vendors, but only 2 to 3 percent led to a purchase order from the home shopping leader.

Despite what appear to be slim odds, I'm here to say that getting on QVC is absolutely feasible. For some, it has been easy. For others, doing business with QVC may take substantial effort. In all cases, however, knowing what your choices are is just as important as understanding the process.

I have been dumbfounded to meet many people that want to be on QVC but have never watched the show. Presenting a product for consideration without finding out what the show is all about, or without researching what similar products may have sold on-air, is akin to applying for a job you know nothing about.

Additionally, many people I've spoken to who have not been able to break into QVC have also only tried once. In my pre-QVC life, I was in the field of energy conservation. Our company sold new technology that would help companies save as much as 70 percent on their utility bills. One day in the office, one of my colleagues and friends called a large manufacturing company about setting up an appointment. After he hung up the phone, I asked him what happened and my friend replied, "The vice president told me to never call him again."

Four months later, my friend called the vice president back, set up an appointment, and closed one of the biggest deals of his career. He told me it was as if the man had never heard of him, that the man was eager to hear what he had to say, and clearly was not the phone slammer he was during their first conversation.

What could have changed during those four months? Maybe the man had a bad day the first time they talked. Maybe my friend had approached him differently the second time. What did happen for sure was that my friend didn't give up. It was his persistence and understanding of how things worked that lead to his success, and I believe the more you work at getting on QVC and the more you know about the process, the better your chances are of getting in the door.

There are a number of ways to get on QVC and this chapter will pull back the veil on the most common.

Mail-in Submission

The short answer to how to get on QVC, and the one that possibly requires the least amount of effort, is to visit www.qvcproductsearch.com, and fill out QVC's online product submission form. The site states that you will receive a response within four to six weeks. QVC requests a photo, brochure, or catalog of your product. You can also send your product along with your application, if you feel it is essential.

For many, this is like sending your headshot to Hollywood, hoping to be in the next installment of *The Godfather*. On the receiving end are piles and piles of photos and resumes that need to be sifted through, deciphered, and organized, much like it would be for absorbing the purpose and possible advantage of a given product.

I often get asked if the mail-in submission process is the best path to getting your product on QVC. My answer is that for many it's the only path, but it's not my favorite. I believe in the personal touch. I believe in forming relationships with people.

In the days when I was not running my own business and looking for a job, I was told that 70 percent of the jobs found by people come from who they know. When trying to get your product on QVC,

I believe the old cliché is true, and knowing someone with connections is likely the best route to getting your product on-air.

I don't doubt in the least that someone at QVC looks at every submission that comes in. I just think that after endless hours of product development on your part, or after traveling the world over for the best diamonds, for example, at the end of the day, there are better ways to pitch your product than by mail.

My own experience also leads me away from this approach, because when I look back I see that many of my ideas and products were so new that submitting them by mail would never have worked.

There is a lot of education involved in presenting a new product to anyone, let alone a buyer. And when relying on written language, a lot gets lost in translation. If you could make a choice between reading directions on how something works, or what it's supposed to do, or how it's supposed to feel against your skin, versus seeing it in person and having it demonstrated to you, what would you choose?

Attend an Open Call

The obvious way to avoid the lack of personal interaction for your product's presentation is to get face to face with a buyer. One of the ways you can do this is to attend an open call, much like the one I described at the opening of this chapter. Regardless of the long lines, at least you will meet with a live body at some point. To find out about the next open call, visit the QVC Web site. At this writing, the section to look for is called How to Become a QVC Vendor.

In the past, these events have included their "50 in 50 Tour," where they covered 50 states in 50 days looking for new items. It can work for you as it has for many others—including a close friend who has now been on QVC for five years and counting. With this approach, you will increase your chances of getting in front of a decision maker who will be able to see and feel your passion while interacting with you about your product.

Networking

Another way to get on QVC is through "who you know," as mentioned before. Network. If someone in your neighborhood or town has been on QVC, call the person. It happens to me all the time. "I'm a friend of a friend of a friend of your cousin's third friend," is how many a call to my office begins. Since QVC has been on air for so many years with so many products, there is likely someone within your proximity who has done it and would be willing to help you in the process of realizing your dream.

Trade Show Marketing

Another way to garner the attention of QVC is by attending a trade show. In many cases, you can make an inquiry to the company running the trade show about prospective or past attendees to see if QVC buyers have or will be in attendance. I have run into QVC buyers at the largest trade shows, as well as many smaller ones that are industry-focused, category-specific.

The problem with trade shows is that the buyers have to find you. And the bigger the trade show, the lower your odds are of getting noticed. It's also a fact that many buyers use the trade show to make appointments with vendors, limiting their time to publicly walk the show.

You can increase your odds of getting noticed at a show, however, by participating in promotions offered by the trade show sponsors. Many such promotions include new product showcases, which short-on-time buyers often peruse to get a glimpse of what is new and worth investigating. (For a list of Top Ten Trade Show Tips, go to www.SellonQ.com/tradeshowtips

You also have the option of thinking outside the proverbial box. I knew of one marketer who bought the side billboard on every bus contracted to carry the trade show attendants from their hotels to the convention center. At the same trade show, one company decided that its best efforts would be to advertise its product in every bathroom.

Another marketer sent a brochure to every house within 25 miles of Wal-Mart's headquarters announcing his company's product and booth number, in hopes of snaring a Wal-Mart buyer. If this is the type of marketing tactic that appeals to you, something similar could be conceived to find the buyer of your choice. The success stories of how people have gotten noticed in the world are countless.

Of course if you have a large staff and have many ongoing promotions in play, you will likely increase your chances of getting noticed at a trade show. Oftentimes a preshow publicity blitz direct to the buyer attendee list provided by the trade show sponsors will increase traffic to your booth, and might land a QVC buyer.

If the trade show is offering a contest, entering it might also boost your profile. That is how one of my colleagues has found more than one product to bring to television. In the very least, non-QVC buyers will notice, and the more attention to your booth the better.

The other problem of hoping to get noticed by QVC at a trade show is that generally buyers from big companies get hounded by eager vendors. If you see someone walking the isle, arms folded, hiding their badge, or their badge is blocked by a business card, it's likely a buyer from a large company. It's a tough situation for them, because everywhere they turn someone wants a piece of them. I've seen in-demand buyers struggle with being able to observe without being pounced on by the overzealous and have come to understand their sometimes less-than-friendly demeanors.

Use an Agent

This brings me to what I believe is the best way to get on QVC, and that is to use an agent. Agents, like QVC buyers, survive based on being successful. They spend a lot of time reviewing and looking for the best products to bring to QVC. They know the rules of the game. They know a lot of buyers and producers, as well as manufacturers. Agents are generally well-connected individuals with keen eyes and ears who can benefit your business in more ways than one.

My first agent used to go out with one of the most popular on-air hosts at the time. He was invited to all the parties and knew everyone there. He lived so close to QVC that he used to go to the studio when they were having cooking shows, along with his newly divorced business partner. The two bachelors would just hang around the set looking for a cooked meal. It's funny to me anecdotally, but they made a lot of connections this way. And that's one of the most important aspects of an agent—their network of people with influence.

When it comes to buyers, any buyer with a brain values the opinion of an experienced agent because they live and breathe in the same environment. Agents are intelligent screens for products. If an agent doesn't understand what it takes to be successful at QVC, they won't survive.

Working with an agent gives you the personal touch needed to effectively reach a buyer with your product. Additionally, they serve as a great sounding board for improving, changing, and creating the perfect presentation. Buyers know this and appreciate it. Simply put, using an agent is miles ahead of the mail-in-say-a-prayer approach.

Picture an everyday occurrence at QVC. A busy agent on appointment with a buyer pitching a new item for a cooking show leaves the meeting. In the hallway, the agent passes by the craft buyer. The agent mentions a new product. "It does this and that, can we get together this afternoon?" "Yes," the craft buyer says. End of story. It's how things get done, not only at QVC but everywhere in the world.

Then the agent decides to go to the QVC cafeteria. It's like high school all over again. Who's sitting with whom? Oh, look, there's "Potsie Weber" (Anson William's character from the old television show *Happy Days*) chatting up his skin care products. Who's that guy with the Toy Buyer? And then the agent sees the Tool Buyer, a friend he plays golf with, and he sets another appointment. It's the high school cafeteria, for sure. Everyone is in everyone else's business, and they all know each other.

I'm painting a picture for you that I've seen a hundred times. Understand that it's not that way for every agent, of course, but relationships get built over time, and success at QVC becomes a community effort. Agents play a vital role in the success of many products that are lucky enough to find airtime on "the Q."

As you might have guessed by now, I'm not only a big fan of agents, but it's the way I got my foot in the door. I was a young guy with a cool little product, and even though I had a background in sales, I knew nothing about retail. I certainly didn't know the first thing about how to approach QVC.

One day I read an article in a magazine about a team of agents who brought products to QVC. I had been mulling over what to do with my new invention and had sent numerous inquiries to companies

I thought might have an interest in licensing or buying it from me. When I read the article about how to get products on QVC, I really didn't think I had a chance so I tossed the magazine aside.

Then, two days later, in another magazine, I read a different article about bringing products to QVC. I read the resource box and I was stunned to see it mention the same team of agents I had just read about days earlier.

Despite the success stories I read about in the article and the various categories of products mentioned, I again pushed it to the back of my mind. I hesitated to contact the agents because I had just been shut out by a handful of major manufacturers in the craft industry after sending out prototypes and introductory letters. If the craft industry was not interested in my product, I didn't see how a mass-merchandising venue like QVC would want it, I reasoned. In my rush to judgment, I thought QVC was about jewelry and household products—not something that would work for a craft-related product like mine.

The universe has a funny way of getting the message across, however, because later in the same week, one of my friends called to ask me if I had any ideas for products that might be right for QVC. I was stunned at the coincidence. How could this be, I asked myself. What are the odds that I would be looking for a way to market my product, read two articles in two different magazines, then suddenly receive a call from my friend asking me about ideas for QVC?

During the conversation, he told me that the small electronics company he worked for had been approached by an agent looking for new items for QVC. My friend thought of me, knowing that I always had a cache of ideas floating around in my fertile mind.

My friend only solidified what was quickly becoming a sign in my eyes, and the three events supported the adage that things come in threes. I was being pulled in the direction of QVC, and I could no longer ignore it, so I decided to call the team of agents from the articles.

In hindsight, I realize that I was biased regarding QVC, and that had an effect on my hesitation to pursue that sales route. At the time it was a fairly new concept, and as a result, mistrusted and the butt of many jokes. It was fairly common to hear people scoff, "Did you see that new show on TV selling jewelry? It looks fake!" Or, "I wouldn't buy anything from that station. They'll be out of business next week!" People were quick to judge, and you could hear any of a variety of negative opinions if the subject came up in conversation. Plus, it was the center of more than one parody on television, and that didn't help my perception of it either. Nobody, it seemed, took the new home shopping channel too seriously.

Fortunately for me, though, it was no joke. I convinced one of the agents from the articles to take a face-to-face meeting, since, I reasoned, "QVC is a visual medium and my product benefits most from a live demonstration." After that, things moved swiftly.

I couldn't believe it. Days before, I doubted the possibility of this avenue for me and my new invention, and then a day after meeting with the agent and his partner, I was sitting in front of two buyers at QVC asking me how fast I could produce 4,000 units.

There are many reasons I'm a believer in a good agent. The first is obvious—they know what they're doing. Not just product-wise, but they know the proverbial ropes more than the average person can understand. They understand the politics of everything from how a product gets positioned to the nuances of pricing.

Quite often, we'll get the previously mentioned phone call to our office from the cousin of a friend of a friend that has a new product. I've represented a few products for others, but generally I try to connect someone to the right agent if I can. I'll tell them my thoughts, and tell them about agents. Then invariably, the caller will ask, "Well, how much is the agent's cut?"

My answer is, a good agent is worth 5 to 10 percent because they'll not only get you in the door based on what and who they know, but they'll likely save your product from extinction at some point. In many ways, they'll pay for themselves.

For example, if you think you want to price your product to QVC at $20 because you want it to sell at retail for say, $40, the truth of the matter is, the agent knows exactly how far they can push the price to meet the retail target you are looking to achieve.

So, if an agent is taking 10 percent, for example, and your thoughts are to sell to QVC for $20 to reach the target of $40, agents should know that they can push it to $22.40, or wherever the break is. So, not only did they pay for themselves but they made you an extra $0.40 per unit. That $0.40 adds up when you're selling 4,000, 10,000, or 20,000 units, or whatever the case may be.

The other way that good agents will pay for themselves is, since they know the rules of the game and the daily on-goings at QVC, they're likely to know what upcoming shows might be right for you. The buyer's daily routine is so busy that despite checks and balances, you and your product might not be at their fingertips.

Buyers might be in the midst of planning a segment and working with a powerhouse of a manufacturer that is presenting dozens of products for their consideration, so that they just might miss you or not make a slot for you.

A good agent's routine includes keeping regular contact with the decision makers and keeping your product "top of mind" for the buyers. The buyers see the agent, and the agent says, "Don't forget so and so for the so and so segment that you have coming up," and that puts you and your product at the top of the buyer's mind.

I had a greedy businessman with a unique product call me up one time. He had a white-knuckle death grip on his pennies, and I could hear them being squeezed on the other end of the phone. Being the nice guy I am, I schooled this man on the workings of QVC, and he scoffed when I mentioned "agent" and "fee."

I explained how agents could pay for themselves based on pricing alone, but then I also asked him to consider what it would be like if an agent was able to secure one more airtime in a twelve-month period than he might be able to secure on his own. Mr. Greedy might be able to pocket an extra $30,000 because the agent knows the upcoming needs of the QVC buyers, but he was too worried about a small percentage that he would have to pay to the agent.

The bottom line is that if you use an agent, build his or her fee into your pricing. Good agents pay for themselves in more ways than one.

Where do you find an agent? Agents, like QVC buyers, are elusive creatures. They scour trade shows, magazines, inventors conventions, and the like, much like QVC buyers. They also write articles, post ads in newspapers, and have Web sites. For more information, visit www.SellonQ.com/qassist.

There is no one place to find an agent but when you do, or if one finds you, consider the following points before commencing a relationship:

- A good QVC agent has a longstanding relationship with QVC of at least five years, with multiple, successful products.
- The agent lives and has an office near QVC (located in West Chester, Pennsylvania, in the suburbs of Philadelphia).
- You should be able to get a list of current or past clients that you can speak with about their experience.
- The agent focuses solely on representing products to QVC.
- The commission should be between 5 and 10 percent of the wholesale selling price to QVC for representation.
- The agent can provide a product demonstrator if necessary.
- You pay the agent after you receive payment from QVC.

I believe physical proximity to QVC is very important for your product's success. Oftentimes, you have a champion for your product in the buying department. Regardless of performance, buyers in general, in any industry, have their favorites. If the buyer leaves his or her position, you have to reacquaint yourself and your product with a new one. An agent who spends a lot of time at QVC will be in a better position to quickly form a relationship with the new buyer. Unfortunately (but sometimes fortunately), the buyer positions at QVC can be a carousel. It's a high-stress position, and turnover is a common and frequent occurrence. In my first few years of dealing with QVC, I would call my agent and the conversations would go something like this:

"Did you have a chance to talk to the buyer about such and such?"

"No, they have someone new over there, Michelle or whoever, left for another department."

We saw something like six buyers in the first two years, and it still happens just as often. So, being close to QVC and knowing the players as they change is vital to maintaining continuity.

Living near QVC also makes it easy to have meetings, attend social functions, and develop relationships with people inside the building.

My first agent has a QVC badge that allows him walk-in access, which he quite often uses just to have lunch in the cafeteria and mingle.

For the same reasons, having an agent that deals exclusively with QVC is also on the top of my list of things to look for. Like anything else in life, if there is a lack of focus, everything suffers. By staying focused on QVC, an agent can sell product in the United States, Germany, and the United Kingdom. These are big opportunities. The only way to stay on top of the QVC market is to specialize.

The agent's commission, for those never having dealt with a sales representative before, is based on your wholesale selling price. For example, if your selling price to QVC is $20, the agent's commission comes from this (and not the on-air selling price). Payment to the agent typically is made after you receive payment from QVC.

In the end, an agent is worth spending the time to find. A good agent knows the life of a product and what numbers you need to maintain. He or she will go to bat for you if you land in a bad segment and your numbers are low as a result. A good agent will protect you from bad airings, too, if possible. Knowing the bell curve of your product and how it's all perceived by QVC, the agent will know when it's time to change or improve your product.

And one thing for certain, a good agent won't let you improve or change your product too soon. In Chapter 15, I show an example where a vendor pulled a successful product well before its time because an overzealous buyer wanted the vendor to make a new and improved version. This untimely decision cost the vendor hundreds of thousands of dollars.

CHAPTER 7

What QVC Looks for in a Product

There is no formula for creating a successful product for QVC, just as there is no formula for determining whether your product will be a success once it gets a chance in the spotlight. There are simply too many variables that affect sales, ranging from timeslots, to what else is on other channels when your item airs, to simply the whim of the buying public.

That said, however, there are things QVC looks for when it entertains new products, and there are ways to ascertain if your product will fit within the scope of QVC.

The more times you can answer yes to the following questions, the greater your chances are of appealing to QVC and its viewers.

- Is your product demonstrable?
- Is your product unique?
- Does your product solve a common problem?
- Does your product have mass appeal?
- Does your product make life easier?
- Is your product brand new to the market?
- Is your product a "better mousetrap"?

Visit www.SellonQ.com/qscore to see how your product rates.

QVC's worldwide warehouse space, according to data provided by QVC at the time of this writing, is the size of approximately 85 U.S. football fields. Its U.S.-based warehouses can pack and ship up to 300,000 packages daily, and annually ship more than a 100 million packages. The retail giant introduces over 1,600 new items every week, in any of the following categories:

- Accessories and shoes
  - Wraps, capelets
  - Fashion jewelry
  - Handbags
  - Intimates
  - Pins
  - Travel and luggage
  - Watches
  - Blazers and jackets
  - Blouses and tops
  - Dresses and sets
  - Maternity
  - Outerwear
  - Pants and skirts
  - Sweaters
  - Swimwear
  - Children's apparel
  - Men's formal wear
  - Men's pants
  - Men's shirts
  - Men's sleepwear
  - Men's sportcoats and blazers
  - Men's suits, sweaters, T-shirts, sweatshirts
  - Team apparel
  - Underwear
  - Men's vests
- Beauty
  - Bath and body
  - Cosmetics
  - Face care
  - Fragrance
  - Hair care
  - Nutritional supplements
  - Relaxation aids

- Jewelry
  - Ankle bracelets
  - Bracelets
  - Charms
  - Children's jewelry
  - Earrings
  - Necklaces
  - Pins
  - Rings
  - Watches
- Cooking and dining
  - Bakeware
  - Cookbooks
  - Cookware
  - Grills
  - Kitchen electrics
  - Kitchen tools
  - Knives
  - Storage and organization
  - Tabletop
- Gourmet food
  - Beef
  - Beverages
  - Fruits and vegetables
  - Gifts
  - Meat
  - Poultry
  - Pork
  - Seafood
  - Snacks
  - Spices and condiments
  - Sugar free
  - Surf and turf
  - Sweets and desserts
  - Weight management
- Home décor
  - Art gallery

- ◆ Bath
- ◆ Bedding
- ◆ Collectibles
- ◆ Decorative accents
- ◆ Flowers and plants
- ◆ Furniture
- ◆ Holiday and party
- ◆ Lighting
- ◆ Mattresses
- ◆ Rugs and mats
- ◆ Sports memorabilia
- Home improvement
  - ◆ Cleaning
  - ◆ Floor care and vacuums
  - ◆ Grills
  - ◆ Home environment
  - ◆ Home projects
  - ◆ Laundry and closet
  - ◆ Lawn and garden
  - ◆ Lighting
  - ◆ Tools
- Electronics
  - ◆ Camcorders
  - ◆ Cameras
  - ◆ Car electronics
  - ◆ Computers
  - ◆ DVD players and VCRs
  - ◆ Home audio
  - ◆ Home office
  - ◆ Movies and music
  - ◆ Phones
  - ◆ Portable electronics
  - ◆ Printers
  - ◆ Software
  - ◆ Telescopes
  - ◆ Televisions
  - ◆ Video games

- Sports and fitness
  - ◆ Athletic apparel
  - ◆ Athletic footwear
  - ◆ Fitness equipment
  - ◆ Fitness videos and books
  - ◆ Health maintenance
  - ◆ Nutritional supplements
  - ◆ Relaxation aids
  - ◆ Sporting goods
  - ◆ Sports memorabilia
  - ◆ Weight management
- Toys, crafts, and leisure
  - ◆ Books
  - ◆ Collectibles
  - ◆ Crafts and hobbies
  - ◆ Games
  - ◆ Movies and music
  - ◆ Pet supplies
  - ◆ Toys
  - ◆ Travel and luggage
  - ◆ Video games
- Holiday
  - ◆ Candles
  - ◆ Christmas figurines
  - ◆ Christmas trees
  - ◆ Chanukkah items
  - ◆ Nativity scenes
  - ◆ Outdoor decorations
  - ◆ Stockings
  - ◆ Table accents
  - ◆ Wreaths and garlands
- Other seasonal items

QVC also sells personalized items such as monogrammed blankets, a piece of furniture that contains your child's name, picture frames, trinket boxes, and so on. If you manufacture personalized items and interfacing directly with customers is the preferred method of operation, understand that QVC has a relationship and reputation with its customers that it strives to protect.

Shipping product directly to QVC's customers is not the normal course of business, but if your product requires specialized care or processing that only you can provide, you may be allowed to ship direct (or *drop-ship*, as it is commonly called).

QVC seeks products with suggested retail prices over $15. This is because it is difficult for a low-priced item to justify the cost of airtime.

For instance, if you have a $10 item and a $20 item, you would have to sell twice as many of the $10 item in order to create the same dollar volume in sales of the $20 item. Generally, this is a more difficult task to accomplish.

If your product has a retail price of less than $15, don't fret. Consider creating a bundle, whether multiples of your item or accessories. For example, if you have a revolutionary cleaning fluid that sells for $9 a bottle; sells multiples; add a package of cloths; add a video for using it on antiques; add a tool for hard-to-reach areas, and so on.

The list of what QVC does *not* sell is much shorter, but is not limited to, the following: firearms, tobacco, tobacco-related products, genuine furs, 900-number phone programs, and programs that contain customer solicitation, such as sweepstakes and questionnaires).

QVC also will not purchase ideas, concepts, or inventions. It is a retailer, and thus looks for manufactured items to sell. It also will not assist you in finding a manufacturer.

In conclusion, preparing and evaluating your product with the things mentioned in this chapter, what you see on-air, and the items found on QVC's Web site, will strengthen not only your product, but your strategic presentation to QVC. If you don't get QVC in your area, you can watch it online at qvc.com.

Your First Meeting—Pitching Your Product for Acceptance

Your first meeting with QVC might well be your only meeting, just as you might only get one chance to impress an agent to take on your product. Careful preparation and research is the key to your success, and creating a presentation that addresses what QVC looks for will increase your odds of getting your product on the number-one home shopping channel in the world.

If your product does not meet the criteria listed in the previous chapter (Is your product demonstrable? Is your product unique? Does your product solve a common problem? Does your product have mass appeal? Does your product make life easier? Is your product brand new to the market? Is your product a better mousetrap?), then perhaps you need to revisit and possibly revamp what you are offering.

Research

People who call our office seeking representation or who simply want an opinion are often so caught up in their product that they don't see it for what it really is. It often reminds me of any number of screenplay seminars I have attended where, invariably, someone in the crowd will raise his hand and say, "What if you've written the greatest screenplay in the world? How do you get it in the right hands?" If the writer gets a chance to share his concept right there on the spot, in most cases, everyone in the crowd can be seen smirking and shaking their head in disbelief. Everyone thinks they have the greatest screenplay, but it's rare that they actually do.

This phenomenon also happens on any given talent show, such as the popular *American Idol.* A contestant sings for the judges. The singer is deplorable. The judges say no. And then the singer leaves in anger because the contestant thinks he or she is a great singer. In some cases, the judges will send contestants on the street with the instruction that if they can bring back ten people who have heard them sing and think they are good, then the judges will give them another chance. It never happens.

The same is true with products. Get an outside opinion—many if possible—and honestly measure your product against the aforementioned questions. Don't delude yourself because you think you have the greatest product since sliced bread. Find out. Step away, ask the hard questions.

If your product is new, do a field test. Set up a table at your local flea market or other sales venue and sell your product. If it doesn't sell at these locations, you likely won't have success at QVC, either. The most discerning opinion you can get is from the buying public.

However, if your product is already selling well, know why it is selling and build that information into your pitch to prospective agents and QVC buyers.

Another important point is, do your research on other products that are similar. Find out if QVC has sold this type of product before by doing a simple search on its Web site. Its Web site does not include products QVC no longer sells, but at least you can find out if it is currently selling something similar.

If it is, you'll have to distinguish your product from the existing product. This can be done in a number of ways, such as price or quality. But if your product is identical to another, you might have to go back to the drawing board and build in a new twist. Also, although you won't be privy to the level of success of the competitive product (an agent might be), it's important to know how the other product is selling. Investigate other avenues, looking for clues to their level of success.

When my agent and I presented the Kreate-a-lope® envelope template to QVC for the first time, we were aware of a previous template collection that had been on air and failed. We used that information by distinguishing our template system from theirs, and as a result, left with a commitment to move forward.

Additionally, your research should include the entire marketplace—outside of QVC. Although many product developers have secured patents, some industries don't merit this level of intellectual property protection. In many cases, it's not conducive to filing a patent when you have a secret formula for your cosmetic line, for example, that will become readily available to all eyes once you file for legal protection. In other cases, people simply don't bother. They create a product and just go for it. Sometimes this can be a disaster. What if the product not only existed before, but also has been patented. By moving forward blindly you'd be infringing on another person or company's patent.

The research is not to be overlooked. You'd be surprised at the number of people who don't know what has been done before them. Just because they haven't seen it doesn't mean it hasn't been attempted.

I found myself watching the first season of the television show called the *American Inventor*. One of the contestants presented her product to the panel, and the response from one of the judges was that the product had been done before and was currently selling in a popular chain store. The contestant was shocked. Offstage, she elaborated on the hours and money she had spent on developing what she thought was her idea. The moral of the story is, do your homework.

The Presentation

So you have your meeting scheduled with QVC: What are you going to say? From my pre-QVC days when I was in corporate sales, I learned three rules:

1. Tell them what you're going to show them.
2. Show them.
3. Tell them what you just showed them.

This framework is designed to keep you focused on your key points. Keep it simple, revolve around your key points, and keep going back to the main elements of your product.

For anyone reading this book who does not have sales experience, I urge you to do some research, purchase a few books on sales, take a course—do anything that will help you to make a killer presentation of your product. Much of sales is also about selling yourself, and a little investment in sales training will go a long way. Go here for a list of recommended materials: www.SellonQ.com/selling.

"Sales 101" dictates that when you want to capture someone's attention, you have to appeal to the emotional need. This is done by illustrating benefits. For example, "This envelope template shows you how to make one-of-a-kind envelopes that your family and friends will rave about next time they get a card or something in the mail from you." The benefit is the emotional connection they will derive from their excited family and friends after they've share a one-of-a-kind custom-made envelope and card with them. It's a connection to happiness, joy, and love.

Certainly, a would-be purchaser is interested in the fact that the template is made from durable plastic and made with precision, but these are features. The key point is, words tell, emotions sell. (For a list of emotional words that sell, visit www.SellonQ.com/powerwords.)

Further, if you were selling lipstick and spoke about the ingredients it contained and the sturdy container it comes in, you likely won't sell many units. Of course, the ingredients are an important part, and many might want to know that the ingredients are safe—but it's not the reason they'll buy.

However, if you spoke about how attractive your lipstick makes a woman feel, how she'll feel when she is wearing it, how long it will last even if she is swimming in the hot sun of a Caribbean hideaway with her partner—these are emotionally based benefits that will be more effective than simply speaking of features.

A QVC buyer, an agent that you meet for the first time, the public that you hope to reach once QVC hands you a big fat purchase order—all of these are people, and all people have emotions. Prepare your presentation to reach them with the emotional benefits of your product and it will help you immeasurably.

Going back to the framework that I use for my presentations, (1) tell them what you're going to show them, (2) show them, (3) tell them what you just showed them. Begin by using an initial benefit statement. For example, "Today I'm going to show you a lipstick that will stay on even after a cool dip in the blue waters of Bermuda."

The questions in a previous chapter about what QVC looks for can be used to your advantage. Use them in your presentation in reverse by presenting your product in light of them. For example,

Does your product solve a common problem?
Illustrate how your product solves a common problem.

Does your product make life easier?
Demonstrate how your product makes life easier.

Is your product a better mousetrap?
Demonstrate how your product is an improvement over another. Demonstrate the innovation that sets you apart from a similar or previous product.

Address each of the questions with an illustration or demonstration. Use the emotions of your product benefits in the forefront of the why's and how's of your presentation. QVC buyers often put themselves in the eye of their consumer. They're often asking themselves the question: Why would I buy this?

Other Helpful Tips for a Great Presentation

- Tap into your passion for the product.
- Know your audience. Research as much as you possibly can about QVC and its product lines. Tailor your presentation to match the information you uncover.
- Stories sell. Tell real-world experiences of people using your product.
- Withhold handouts until the end of the presentation to prevent reading ahead and to allow your audience to draw their own conclusions.
- Include sales data or information about past successes that are pertinent to being successful on QVC.
- Answer the question in the buyer's mind: Why would I buy this product?

Use stories to make the emotional connections of your product real. My first product on QVC was the envelope template I've mentioned before. Unbeknownst to me at the time, my agents were looking at my template with the experience of knowing that a year prior to my meeting with them, QVC had already had an envelope template on-air that had failed.

Fortunately, mine was, in their words, a better mousetrap. At the time I was naïve about the fact that there were other templates out there, but I knew what made mine fun for people, and I conveyed it to my agents and QVC emotionally.

Unknowingly I addressed how mine solved the problems that the failed envelope template couldn't. My template didn't require scissors. My template didn't require a pencil for tracing. It produced immediate results and this ease was the vehicle for my emotional end result—sharing with family and friends something you could make in 15 seconds or less.

(Check it out: www.GreenSneakers.com/envelope.)

Make your presentation an emotional connection, and it will take you a long way. Remember, words tell, emotions sell.

The QVC Mindset

In addition to emotional selling, it is important to understand what makes QVC successful. QVC stands for quality, value, and convenience. If you don't address these issues, whether directly or indirectly, in your meetings with QVC buyers or with agents, you may be left to wonder why QVC hasn't accepted your product. It is first in the home shopping business for many reasons, and this three-letter acronym is credited for much of its success.

Quality

Make sure you manufacture a quality product. Show evidence in your pitch that this is so. If you're pitching with a prototype bring a finished sample of a similar product made by your company, or your manufacturer, that establishes the benchmark you will be using in manufacturing your final product for QVC.

Value

QVC strives to offer its customers the best value/price for the products it sells. If you sell your item in a major retail store and you bring it to QVC, make sure the buyers know it's in the marketplace already—first and foremost—but also, make sure they QVC is getting the best price.

If you can't work the price to be the lowest for QVC, then reconfigure the product so it's tailor-made for QVC's customers. This is a common practice in the world that allows a manufacturer to sell virtually identical product lines to competing stores by making each slightly different than the other. Perhaps you can add or remove an accessory that comes with your item, change the size, improve the product, or make some other minor change.

Furthermore, along the lines of pricing, know a few things going in. The majority of their categories work in the framework of buying product at approximately 50 percent of the proposed retail cost. This is what is known as *keystone pricing*.

QVC also has a second formula that it uses for products it plans to sell at an introductory price (IP). If you watch the show, you will often see a QVC price with a slash through it, then below it the words "introductory price" and a lower price next to it.

The IP number is generally 8 to 10 percent lower than the regular price and only stays that way for the first 13 appearances before going back to the higher price. Not all products get an IP. This is a decision made by programming and not on the buying level. Even though you have no control over whether your product will get an IP, it is important information for strategizing your selling prices to QVC.

Convenience

Although ease of shopping on QVC with its automated systems is one way to look at the convenience QVC refers to and strives to achieve, addressing the convenience of your product is also an important point to make in your presentation. It's simply a way to restate why your product is a better solution than the status quo, and how owning it will make life easier for people.

As a final word on presenting your product to QVC for success, remember that QVC is a visual medium. The more you can convey visually, the easier it will be to understand and respond to your product and the easier it will be for the buyers to make a yes decision. A demonstration is worth a thousand words. Make sure yours is simple, concise, and shows the *wow* factor of your product.

CHAPTER 9

Your Product Has Been Accepted—Now What?

Congratulations! Your product has received the green light from QVC and you're on your way. Hopefully, everyone was correct and you and your product have what it takes to be an incredible success. If your product has not been accepted yet, skip this chapter and come back to it when you're ready.

Most strangers that I encounter think that once you land on QVC, you become an instant millionaire. It is not that simple, even though becoming a millionaire in one day is certainly possible. Mostly, it takes time and perseverance, along with quality products, to be successful on television.

Much of the hard work happens once your product gets accepted. Hopefully, you have a staff of helpers. If you don't, don't worry. With the right guidance and careful planning, you'll make your deadlines.

A common question by new vendors is, how much product will QVC order? There is no specific answer, and it depends on many variables. For example, if you're famous and the product has already been successful in other outlets, then your order might be very large and a special promotion might be created just for you. If you're an average company, an opening order might be just enough to test the product. You also might be put in an overnight spot to see if there is a demand.

Many first orders are prepped for a retail sale in the area of $50,000 to $75,000. (Overnight test spots are prepped for much less.) What this means is that if your item is going to have a retail price of $25, and QVC is targeting $50,000 in retail sales, then you will get an order for 2,000 units ($50,000 divided by $25).

Another important question involves manufacturing. In most cases, your product is shipped to any one of QVC's numerous warehouses well in advance of your on-air date. This allows QVC to inspect the merchandise for quality and also insures that all customer orders are shipped immediately. Expect to have to ship product four weeks before your air date.

The Product Submission Process

The remainder of this chapter is an overview of the product submission process. It is designed to help alleviate the potential angst that many feel once they begin the process and to help you gain familiarity with what will be expected of you as a QVC vendor.

Once you become a QVC vendor, you will receive a welcome packet with complete and up-to-date information. The other component that you will be privy to is access to QVC's vendor Web site. It contains everything you are required to know, guidelines for shipping, product labeling, packaging, invoicing information, product descriptions, preferred vendor lists for shipping, and bar code label creation information. This is not available to the general public. You need to be assigned access information, and this happens once QVC accepts your product and you get your first purchase order.

Inside the vendor Web site, you will also be able to check on the status of your item after submitting it to the quality assurance department. You will also be able to check on inventory, sales stats, purchase orders, payments made by QVC, and so on. It's the central hub where you will find most of your answers.

Here is an overview of basic requirements:

Long description form. This form begins the internal process. It generates an item number from which a purchase order will be created. The long description form contains the description that will be used in the QVC database. In addition to being used by QA, buyers, and planners, it will be used to develop the online description for when your product appears in QVC's retail Web site. It is composed of 8 lines, 70 characters per line. It also asks for a suggested four-line description, the *product dubner*. Next time you watch QVC look at the product description on the left side of the screen. It will usually be four lines, and each line is limited to 13 characters.

Additionally, you will need to include a manufacturer's item number, item cost, and several other pieces of information that you negotiate with your buyer, such as *return to vendor* percentages and customer returns.

Vendor information sheet. This form also needs to be submitted before you receive a purchase order. It contains company information, remit to address, ship from address, returns address, and so on. This form sets you up in QVC's computer system.

Liability insurance. Currently, the liability insurance requirement is $1,000,000, with QVC listed as certificate holder. Carriers must be "acceptable to buyer"—AM Best-rated A or better. Vendor shall maintain above minimum coverages for the life of the merchandise. (Check out Free Resources on www.SellonQ.com.)

Claims substantiation policy. This is a lengthy form that you must read and sign. QVC requires that any claim you make about your product be backed up by scientific data. This pertains to written and spoken (on-air) claims.

Vendor bounceback forms (if applicable). QVC frowns on what it terms a *bounceback*. A bounceback is when you include information in your product that attempts to solicit customers. One example of a bounceback is something you might include in your product directions: "For more information, please visit our Web site, www.GreenSneakers.com." You are allowed to include your company name, address, Web site, phone numbers, and so on, but asking for customers to contact you requires approval and a signed vendor bounceback form that states you will not attempt to solicit customers you acquire from your dealings with QVC.

Warranties. If applicable, you will be required to supply warranty copies for your product.

Quality assurance (QA) sample submission form. This contains your product information, along with a bullet list of forms and documents you must submit with your product to your buyer, who, in turn, submits them to QA.

QVC's quality assurance department has extremely rigorous standards. Expect to be rejected. Expect to find compromises. The individuals in this department have children, husbands, wives, and family like the rest of us, and they strive to protect them as stringently as they desire to protect QVC's customers from defective and inferior products. They take their jobs very seriously, but they do listen and will work with you. Many people groan about the QA process. Know that they are not your enemy—persevere.

Tips to Prepare for Success

- Establish trusted relationships with your vendors; establish credit with them early.
- Establish other lines of credit.
- Know your manufacturing limits and plan for lead times accordingly.
- Know your plan if you get a big order.

Creative Financing in Action

On one of our large early orders, QVC was interested in 25,000 units. Good news, except one thing—we didn't have the $200,000 required to manufacturer that many pieces. Fortunately, I had begun establishing credit and had good relationships with my vendors, but it wasn't enough.

I formulated a plan. I approached all my vendors and asked them to extend their normal 30-day payment terms to 60 or 90 days, if possible. I then asked them all if I could pay by credit card, and they all said yes. My plan was to roll the $200K for as long as possible, and when it came due, I would pay each bill using my various credit cards, which by this time had about $100,000 total in available credit.

I figured I could get an extra 60 days on top of what my suppliers were giving me by paying any bills after the closing date of my credit card. For example, one of my credit cards closed on the twenty-first of each month. By using this card to pay a bill after that day—say, the twenty-second of the month—I would get an additional 60 days before I would have to pay the credit card its money because the next statement wouldn't come out for another month, and that bill wouldn't be due for another 30 days after that.

By using this technique, along with the extended terms I was being given by my suppliers, I was going to be able to postpone payment on $200,000 for as long as 150 days. I was banking on selling most, if not all, of the items, and this strategy would give me plenty of time to receive payment from QVC in order to pay my suppliers. The great news is, I didn't have to use it. We sold everything, and QVC paid us within 30 days of the airing.

Technically, once your product has been approved by QVC's quality assurance department, you can begin manufacturing. If you begin manufacturing before final approval, though, you might find yourself in a position of having to rework your product because QA wants you to make a change in your directions, or might find that one of your components doesn't meet QVC's specifications. Maybe your packaging needs to be improved, for example. I have been in precarious positions regarding fast-approaching air dates and manufacturing lead times. Be forewarned that this is risky territory. Therefore, I recommend waiting until QA approves your product before manufacturing.

10

How to Prepare for Your Big Moment on TV

This chapter is critically important to your success. How you think through and prepare your presentation will be a strong indicator of how you will perform in front of the camera.

The Backyard Fence

My first appearance on television was nerve-wracking. I didn't have any training, didn't know what to expect, and had only demonstrated my product to a live body less than a hundred times. I didn't have a clue about many things, and needless to say, my on-air performance left a lot to be desired. Fortunately, I knew my product very well, and the demonstration of the product spoke for itself. We did sell our entire inventory, despite my shortcomings.

The information that follows will erase many of the unknowns for you and will help you prepare for your on-air success. It is built on the many things I've learned from being on-air nearly two hundred times in four countries and selling on the trade show circuit in countless cities around the world.

This chapter also contains many things I've learned from training others to demonstrate products for television sales over the last ten years. Here you will also gain insight into the QVC selling philosophy and the training it provides for first-time vendors.

Nowadays QVC requires every new on-air sales person to attend a Guest Excellence Seminar. It's a two-part training that provides you with a foundation for your on-air appearance. The first part is completed online from home. The second part is an all-day event that takes place at QVC headquarters.

The training covers QVC's sales philosophy, which I explain later in this chapter, and provides often-overlooked details on where to go for support, what to do when you arrive the day of your airing, general protocol, and legal and claims requirements. Participants also fine-tune their pitches with the help of others in the group before working with one of the actual QVC hosts in a taped mock television presentation. Afterward, a TV sales mentor will discuss your performance with you.

I would like to clear up the use of the word *sell* when used throughout this and other chapters. I don't believe in the word per se when it comes to being on-air. I use it because it is understood by many. When I present a product, whether on television or at a trade show, I rarely think of it as selling. I prefer to look at it as sharing and demonstrating with passion. When I discuss what I like about the item and what it can do, people can observe without feeling like they are being sold something.

Fortunately, my philosophy falls in line with QVC's. It professes a friendly *backyard fence* approach to selling where you are a friend of the host and everyone is watching. This makes the viewers feel like they are watching neighbors having a conversation about a product over the backyard fence.

Keeping it warm and friendly becomes a challenge when you are on-air because you have to juggle your presentation with a professional host at your side, there is limited time, there are various camera positions to be aware of and two monitors to keep an eye on, and an occasional caller that will ask questions or talk about your product while you are in the middle of your demonstration, for example.

The more you know about what to expect and how to prepare, the more relaxed you will be when your time in front of the camera finally arrives.

Bullet Points

You likely know your product so well that you can speak about it for hours. Knowing your product intimately and being able to speak about it with passion is the key to success.

However, the format of QVC is time-limited, so it is very important to rein yourself in. A very good way of doing this is to develop three key points about your product that you can revolve around during your presentation. Of course, you can deviate and expand, but having three key points provides for a strong foundation for both you and the host and also keeps things simple for the viewers, making them more likely to make a purchase.

The first time you first arrive at QVC for an on-air segment, you'll be asked to fill out a blue card that asks for your three points as they relate to your product. This card is shared with the host so you are both on the same page.

In Chapter 8 I wrote about conveying your product in terms of benefits, the importance of tapping into the emotional element. This is even more important when presenting your product on-air, and for this reason should be incorporated into your three key points.

For example, if you were selling a digital camera, your three key points could be as follows:

1. **Turns on with no delay:** "This camera turns on in an instant, so next time you want to capture your son or daughter in a precious moment you won't miss the shot."
2. **Clear and crisp photos:** "This camera takes clear, crisp digital photos so if you wanted to enlarge and print one of your new baby, it will still be clear and crisp."
3. **Auto settings:** "The auto settings on this camera let you focus on capturing the memory of the moment without you trying to remember how to use the buttons."

A confused mind always says, "No," so keep it simple and appeal to people's emotions.

Broaden Your Market Reach

The only on-air training I had before my first demonstration occurred about ten minutes before I was going on-air for the first time. My agent pulled me to the side of the green room and had me watch a man selling a siphon on one of the studio televisions. (QVC didn't have the training it offers now.)

When most people hear *siphon* they think about siphoning gas out of a car. Well, this man was selling a better mousetrap of a siphon that worked with a hand pump, but he wasn't just selling it to one group of people, he was selling it to outdoors lovers, housewives, handymen, just about anyone.

His demonstrations included how the siphon could be used to transfer gas from a boat to a can for storage. He showed how you could use the siphon to transfer wine from one barrel to the next. He showed how you could use it in the home, in the garage, or out in the middle of a lake. He demonstrated a lot of applications and showed how women, men, and even children were capable of applying his unique siphon to just about anything with a fluid in it.

Additionally, because he was demonstrating such a wide variety of uses, he was giving people a reason for buying more than one. Customers would not want to use the same siphon in the kitchen that they used in the garage.

The lesson I gained from the "siphon guy" helped me broaden my own market reach by thinking about all the people that could benefit from my products. It is something I brainstorm about every time I create a new presentation. It is invaluable.

Using this technique can open a new demographic or give more people a reason to buy. And this can mean the difference between selling 3,000 or 4,000 units. I encourage you to make it a regular part of your on-air brainstorming sessions and training. Getting a new product on QVC is challenging enough, so use this exercise to sell more of what you already have in the pipeline and positively impact your bottom line.

Train at Home

When my company trains people for on-air sales, we set up a mock scenario including cameras, demonstration table, a monitor, a host, and a testimonial caller or two. Your setup at home needn't be this elaborate to be effective. At the very least, work with a family member or friend. Have them play the host while you work through the sale.

Your mock-host's job is to introduce you, to ask you questions, to "play rough" at times by trying to dominate the conversation, and to close out the segment. Work for four to six minutes and also for eight to ten minutes at a clip. These are the likely time limits you will have when you actually go on-air.

Creating a staged practice like this will help you gain confidence and verbal flow. Practice, practice, practice. On the athletic field, they say, how you perform in practice is how you will perform on the field.

Field Training

I can't stress field training enough. If you have the opportunity to sell to a live crowd whether at a mall kiosk, a consumer trade show, county fair or any other event, do it. Being able to see why and when a person makes a buying decision is extremely beneficial and can easily be incorporated into your on-air demo.

Shortly after my first on-air appearance, I discovered consumer trade shows. I'm referring to the kind of show where you have a booth and you sell directly to the attendees of the trade show and they take the product with them on the spot. They're a step or two above a flea market in that they're usually targeted to a certain interest group and they're supported by advertising budgets and the like.

They're also in contrast to industry wholesale trade shows where store owners and buyers attend to place orders with manufacturers to be shipped at a later date.

Contrary to the often-slower tempo of a wholesale trade show, consumer trade shows are usually fast paced and crowded. As a demonstrator in this environment, you have limited chances to gain and maintain someone's attention because there is so much for the consumer to see and do.

There's a reason why comedians have been given their own sitcoms. They're funny and they've tested their material in front of live audiences. In many interviews I've seen with comedians, they'll often discuss how switching around a punch line is the difference between getting a big laugh or no laugh at all. The same is true in face-to-face sales.

When real money is at stake, your senses become attuned to buyer impulses. The takeaway point is, listen, learn, adapt, change, tweak, and then repeat until you're maximizing your effectiveness and are able to sell your product consistently well to all types of people.

Being on the road and selling directly to the public allowed me to develop a three-step demonstration process that I use to this day for my envelope templates. I was able to see what made people standing right in front of me reach in their pockets for their wallet.

This type of field training causes you to think on your feet. Oftentimes you will come away with a catch-phrase or a new idea after demonstrating for an eight-hour stretch. You might even get your money-making phrase from one of the visitors to your booth.

In any event, working in front of a live group will definitely help your verbal delivery and build your confidence, which will undoubtedly affect your numbers in a positive way.

Long Demonstrations

If you have a long demonstration, you have a problem. With all the handshaking, intros, callers, and unpredictable tangents, your on-air time will be over before you know it. Fortunately, there are generally two solutions to shortening a long demonstration. The first is to do a *step-process*. The second is to prepare a *B-roll.*

A step-process is where you break down your demonstration into steps, taking the longer ones and creating a setup and a finished result, so you can abbreviate the time it takes to go from one to the other.

A good example of this can be found in just about any cooking segment. For example, the turkey is stuffed and seasoned, and then placed in the oven. The time and attention is given to the seasoning of the turkey, while the cooking time is accelerated when the host pulls a finished turkey from under the counter to show you the end result.

You can prepare a step-process for just about anything. Common mistakes to avoid include leaving out important steps and assuming your viewers know what you are doing when, in most likelihood, they're seeing it for the first time. Be clear and explain your missing steps clearly.

The other way of speeding up your demonstration is to use a B-roll. A B-roll is auxiliary video footage prepared in advance that shows time-lapsed steps of your process. In other words, with the power of editing you can control time, speed, and camera angles to the benefit of clearly explaining what your product does in less time than it actually takes to do it. Often, a B-roll is invaluable and must be used.

QVC, however, is a live broadcast. By presenting a product live, it adds to your credibility. QVC strives to be live, so try to work out your demonstration before going down the path of using a B-roll.

It is important to know that before producing a video for on-air use, you must consult with QVC and obtain permission. And even after you have their permission, they reserve the right to allow or disallow your video, as well as the right to edit it before putting it on-air. Lastly, you must submit your finished video for approval prior to your on-air appearance.

Here are a few guidelines for what makes a good B-roll for QVC:

- It shows a demonstration or part of a demonstration that cannot be executed effectively live.
- It does not contain text or graphics.
- It reflects the style and brand of QVC.
- It is 30 to 45 seconds in length.
- It highlights the most important points first.

A video that contains graphics, has poor acting, shows a demonstration that you're doing live, or has an infomercial style to it, will likely be rejected by QVC.

Furthermore, according to QVC's vendor guidelines, it will not accept video that contains scrolls, text graphics, taped testimonials, or "quad" screen footage (four different scenes showing on one screen). QVC currently accepts beta SP or digital beta tapes. Tapes mastered on lower-quality mediums such as VHS and then submitted on beta will not be accepted.

To see an example of a B-roll visit www.SellonQ.com/broll.

If you want to produce a video for your segment but do not know how to go about it, QVC has a division called Product Works that can assist you. Once you establish a relationship with QVC, you will have this resource available to you.

Stories Sell

If you have stories about your product from your personal life, consider sharing them with the viewing audience. Stories generate interest and convey many things, such as trust and examples of usage. People love to hear them, and they are effective sales tools.

How to Dress for Television

Clothing

If you are impeccable in your appearance, it will raise your credibility. The most effective look is professional and contemporary. Dress to match the level of professionalism called for by your product and industry. Jewelry experts, dress fashionably, and have manicured hands if holding samples; tool demonstrators, dress with clean, collared shirts and new jeans; computer experts, wear collared shirts, possible jacket and tie, and so on. V-neck shirts and blouses both open and balance your appearance. Avoid turtlenecks and other high-collared tops. They truncate your look and often give the appearance of a floating head. Avoid wrinkled clothes. Select colors that contrast with your skin tone and hair color. Vivid colors are generally better than muted earth tones. Avoid white and don't wear plaid or clothing with stripes.

Hair

Keep you hair neat. Avoid extremes in style. Men, get a clean shave; if bearded, be well groomed.

Makeup

Makeup is optional but recommended. If skin makeup is used, match your skin tone. For oily and shiny skin, use an oil-absorbing powder. If using lipstick or blush, select tones bright enough to shine through bright stage lighting.

Visual Image

Creating a consistent and powerful visual image in the form of your appearance is akin to branding your product. Think through your choices wisely.

Testimonial Calls

If you watch QVC, quite often you will hear a testimonial caller. These are not staged calls but, rather, callers picked at random from the telephone sales queue. What will happen is a viewer will call in to buy the item being demonstrated, and randomly the QVC operator will ask if callers want to go on-air.

Another way this happens is the QVC host will ask viewers to call in if they've ever used the product. These individuals are then selected by the operators to go live and, when the appropriate time comes, will be able to speak to the host and the guest.

A *testimonial call (T-call)* is a powerful sales tool. Accept it and work with it. I used to get mad at testimonial calls because they would interrupt the flow of my demonstration and seemed to take too much time. That was before I learned how to work with them and how vital they were to increasing sales. Now I recognize their importance and I welcome them.

The reason T-calls are effective is because they offer what is commonly know in sales circles as *social proof*. T-calls let viewers hear what people like (and don't like) about a product that they've purchase and how they've used it in their own lives. A T-call is like a neighbor joining in on the backyard fence conversation that you've been having with the host.

The Internet giant, Amazon.com, uses its own version of QVC's T-call in the form of customer testimonials placed on its site in written text. It has even taken it one step further to cross-promote other items with its feature "customers that purchased this item also purchased these items." Amazon's success is testimony that social proof works.

The best way to work with a testimonial call is to listen to what the callers are saying and respond to them. Many times, you'll be surprised what they say, and you might even learn of new ways to use your product.

One time, I was in the middle of a demonstration when we took a phone call from a woman who said she used every product we ever made. She went on to say that on a typical Friday night her family will get together and use our products to make gifts for others. At the end of the demonstration, my wife ran out on the set, not to tell me that we sold out, but to remark at the phone call.

Imagine how we felt knowing a family somewhere in the country was affected so positively with our products, not to mention how her call to QVC that day likely affected our sellout and reputation with other viewers. People respond to stories with an emotional impact, and if you receive a T-call you might just get an emotionally charged story.

The importance of a T-call can't be stressed enough. If you don't let the caller speak or ignore the caller, your disrespect will come across to the viewers. Obviously, this is not a good thing. It will look like you are not listening, and your sales will suffer.

Sometimes the callers wander off the topic and this can be frustrating to the inexperienced demonstrator, but it lends to the conversational nature of the call and often times results in more testimony from the caller. The hosts know what to do and when to take over the call if it's a runaway, so my best advice is to go with the flow.

When a T-call comes in, what the viewing audience typically sees is a two-shot of you and the host, plus your display. Stop your demonstration and look into the camera when you speak to the caller, it's like making eye contact with someone when you're with them in person. If the conversation is about something to do with your product, demonstrate it as you would to someone in your own home if it feels right.

Some on-air demonstrators try to control the flow of a T-call by redirecting the conversation. This, in most cases, is bad form and comes across like selling and should be avoided. It also demonstrates that you're simply not listening to the caller.

Another example of something *not to do* is to try to control who calls in as a testimonial call in the first place. Guests and vendors are strictly prohibited from attempting to stage testimonial phone calls, and it is a serious violation of QVC's policies. It's bad for you, it's bad for QVC, and it's bad for other vendors.

T-calls are phenomenal sales tools and come from people that could be someone's grandmother. Respect them, listen to them, roll with the flow, and you will see the results in your sales.

A Typical Segment

This section covers a typical presentation as I have experienced them and provides tips on what to expect along with advice on what to do and what not to do. Incorporate this knowledge into your practice sessions or your mental preparation so you don't get blindsided by any unknowns.

The QVC set is composed of a number of cameras and two monitors. Sometimes there are as many as three cameras on the floor that are remotely controlled and one stationary overhead camera if needed. Sometimes a camera on a boom is also used. A *boom* is a long moveable arm that has a camera attached to the end. It is used for overhead shots and stylistic moving shots. Quite often you will also find a handheld camera with a mobile operator being used for difficult close-up angles.

There are two monitors on the floor, or hanging above the floor, in front of the demonstration area, acting as a pair. They will be moved into view when the demonstration begins.

The monitor on the right shows what is happening as the viewer sees it, live. The monitor on the left shows what is coming up as the producers prepare the next shot. It might be a close-up, static product shot or something else pertinent to the demonstration.

The left monitor also contains information such as the name of the testimonial caller about to be introduced if there is one and the city and state they live in. It also displays how much time is remaining in your segment.

The best way to work with the monitors is to glance at them quickly. If you see that your eyes or face are not being shown, then look at the monitors for what information you need.

If you watch David Letterman, you might have noticed a segment where he talks with Rupert, the owner of the Hello Deli. Watch Rupert—he is always looking toward the ground. Regardless of whether they use monitors for this segment or not, Rupert's long looks to the ground depict what it looks like when someone is watching themselves in a monitor. It's distracting to the viewer and shows a lack of professionalism, so be quick with a glance before staring at them.

Prior to going on-air you will need to be fitted with a *Lavaliere microphone* and an *earpiece*. The small microphone is attached to your shirt or blouse with a clip. This is so the viewer can hear what you are saying. The earpiece allows you to hear the callers or the producer should they need to instruct you while you are on-air. The earpiece and microphone are attached to separate transmitting units that attach to your clothes out of view of the television audience.

Once on the set, most segments begin with a two-shot/master shot of you and the host along with your display. The host will then begin speaking about your product and will segue into introducing you. A *master shot* is film and television talk meaning to frame the set in the camera in its entirety. A two-shot is when there are two people in the frame. For QVC purposes the master shot usually is the two-shot.

After your introduction, one of the cameras will typically feature a close-up of you. (The camera with the red light on top is the one that is live at the moment.) This gives the viewers a chance to see you and begin to get to know you.

In the close up, I just try to be natural. Sometimes I look in the camera and smile as if I'm seeing a friend. I try not to stare, and I don't pressure myself to maintain a look into the camera. Other times if the host and I are bantering back and forth at that moment, then I look at the host and continue as I normally would. If you're ever in doubt about what to do, think "backyard fence."

It's interesting to watch a show like ESPN, where the hosts are clearly instructed to begin conversing with each other in the master shot and then, once the new speaker gets going, the camera changes to a one-shot of the speaker's face while he or she turns to speak directly into the camera—while their fellow announcers are actually right beside them. It's awkward to the person doing it because it's not naturally how you converse with people next to you, but it involves the viewer as if they were in the group having the conversation, too.

In any event, the close-up on you is barely ten seconds. From there the host might introduce your product and what it contains. If you have a display board, you might be asked to discuss the contents of your product. One of the cameras will likely be focused on the board in a close-up to provide the best view. Use the live monitor to pace your movements as the camera pans and tilts across your display because you want what you're saying to be synchronized with what is being shown to the viewers.

After the product overview, it's time for the demonstration. Depending on your product, sometimes the demonstration comes before the product overview. From here a variety of things can happen. You might receive a testimonial call or a static shot of your product might be displayed on the screen. If you're using a B-roll, it might be shown at this point as well. Much of what happens is determined by how much time you have been allotted.

As your segment winds down, you might hear the producer in your earpiece telling you to wrap it up. The host then summarizes your product and thanks you for coming.

If you follow the tips in this chapter and practice at home, in the field, and participate in QVC's training, you will ease a lot of otherwise unnecessary anxiety. Tension translates to the viewers and can be avoided by gaining confidence through repetition and putting yourself through dynamic environments of the demonstration process.

As a sidebar to your sales preparation, consider the QVC audition process for would-be hosts. At one time, as part of the interview process, prospective candidates for hosting would be handed a pencil and asked to sell it for five minutes! What could you say about a pencil that would entice someone into buying it while appearing natural and fun loving?

11

A Day in the Life at QVC

Most people think I, or any of my contemporaries, show up at the studio, go on air, make a million dollars in ten minutes, jump in the car, and go home. I'm sorry to say that there is a lot more to it than that.

A typical day at QVC for me begins a few days before my on-air date. I receive a phone call from the TV sales manager to discuss anything from sales strategies to broadcasting logistics. The conversation can cover the use of a handheld camera during the sell to the nuts and bolts of my setup. We might discuss things like what size table might I need or if I need an easel for my display.

The TV sales manager also provides times for when I need to be in the studio, my tentative on-air time, and what host I am tentatively scheduled to work with and when the host will be available to meet with me.

Because QVC is a live broadcast, many things can change—thus, the tentative information. A product scheduled for your hour might sell out in an earlier appearance. An on-air guest may not arrive. Martha Stewart might decide at the last minute that she doesn't want to appear at 8 p.m. because the president of the United States is scheduled to make a major announcement and everyone scheduled in the 7 p.m. hour might have to switch to the 8 p.m. hour and take the hit for Martha (true story).

At QVC, just about anything can happen, so everything has a tentative notation attached to it.

I live within driving distance of QVC, so, depending on my airtime, I might arrive the night before and stay over, or I might drive there on the same day. In any case, I usually have to arrive at the studio anywhere from two to four hours in advance. This is so I can meet with the host before his or her scheduled shift to go over my product and planned demonstration, and to answer any questions. The hosts are always prepared, having reviewed the products they will be working with thoroughly in advance.

Once I arrive at QVC's headquarters in West Chester, Pennsylvania, I check in with security. After getting my badge, I make my way to the studio operations desk to let them know I've arrived. They hand me a pager so I can be notified. This could be to let me know that the host is ready to meet with me or when they're ready to get me ready for going on air with the necessary electronics.

I am also required at this time to sign any releases for use of my image and name on air, or any related promotions, releases for any photographs I plan on using, or any video I've provided, and so on. Here I also fill out an information card about my product if it is new to QVC.

Next up, I have to check in with FMV—full motion video/digital imaging. This is where the on-air product shot is created. This is the still photo that is used for any previews and during the presentation.

My products have a lot of components and convey better when displayed on a board, so I make sure to arrive well in advance. It makes it easier for the people running FMV, and I prefer this type of display.

If FMV is in a time crunch or if I don't arrive until the last minute, they will work directly with the product itself and make it look as good as possible. This works for jewelry and other products but, since we have a lot of pieces, I prefer using a vertical board planned well in advance.

Once we have the laser shot completed for my on-air static product shot, I look for the coordinating producer. This is the person who runs the studio floor. He or she communicates and clarifies legal claims for hosts and guests, maintains the production values, and communicates key strategies and points of execution to the live crew. The coordinating producer manages guests in the studio and is the liaison between the line producer and the studio floor (the line producer is the "captain of the ship" and directs all elements of the show).

The coordinating producer knows when and where my segment will take place, and this information determines where and when I can set up. In the main studio, QVC has at least a dozen sets or stages, from bedroom sets to living rooms to a garage set to any number of kitchen sets. There is a set for everything and anything.

The original studio had a round stage with pie-shaped stages within. When your segment was coming up the crew would rotate the entire set so that you would be in front of the few cameras they had at the time. It was like being a pizza getting rotated in the oven so you would cook on all sides, but you had to hold on to your toppings as the stage turned, lest your anchovies spill over on the floor seconds before going live! They've come a long way since then.

Once my setup is complete, I head over to the green room to see who else is scheduled for the day. In the green room, you'll usually find a bevy of unique characters, people from all walks of life, all with a different story to tell.

At this time, if you're so inclined, you might make a trip to hair and make-up. It's not required, but many elect to take advantage of this. Make your appointment before your on-air day.

QVC's green room is not only a place to relax prior to your segment, it is a place to see what is happening sales-wise. In addition to the televisions in the room showing the current broadcast, they have several computers. Most friends that I've taken to QVC are amazed at the computers and the data they display. They are the pulse of the show and contain information on all the products in a given hour.

The information available to us includes beginning inventory of any item, sales per unit, how many sales there are of multiple units, how many first-time-ever buyers there are (these are people who never bought anything from QVC before), total units, and how many operators are receiving orders in any of four call centers. There are graphs indicating call volume, the amount of callers on the lines at any given time, and more.

The information is beneficial for anyone who knows how to interpret and use it. For example, on the graph that indicates the call volume, you might see a spike where the inbound calls jumped from 400 to 1,253. If you have been watching the presentation at the same time, you might know what caused the spike. It might have been something the guest said. It might be a strong testimonial call. The information you can gain from this is as close to a face-to-face sell as you can get, where you see why someone reaches in their pocket to buy.

Take the data from the computers and use it next time to better your performance. Perhaps it was part of the demonstration that caused the spike. Next time, you'll know to get to the demonstration quicker.

One time I correlated a spike to a comment that came over my earpiece from the producer while in the middle of my segment. He asked me to show something again. Later, my agent told me we had a large spike on the graph, and we figured it happened during the part of the demonstration I was asked to repeat. The real-time information is invaluable to everyone, from the producers to the guests.

People ask me all the time if the sales numbers QVC sometimes displays are accurate. They are referring to the numbers that occasionally show up on your television screen at the bottom when a product is selling well. The answer is yes with an asterisk, because the numbers you see on the screen are actually behind by several hundred.

I've been told that the information being broadcast on television must be truthful or the broadcaster risks being fined by the regulatory authority known as the Federal Communications Commission (FCC). So, in order to stay in compliance, the sales numbers that are being shown to the public are actually lower than the actual sales taking place.

The on-screen sales numbers only appear when a product is selling very quickly or near a sellout. This makes sense because this is known to create two things that are proven to drive sales—scarcity and social proof (something approved by many, which in sales is measured when a lot of people buy) so it makes sense to show the numbers when an item is really moving fast or about to run out.

At last, the host is ready to meet with me. It's informal, and most often happens on the set where I've already set up my display. We go over my product, I show the host the demonstrations I have planned, the host asks questions and makes a suggestion or two of how we'll begin. All the while, the host is making notes on the blue card used on air that contains my product's description, price, and item number. And then the host is off to meet with the next guest.

I wait.

Finally, I get buzzed on my pager that they gave me when I first arrived. It's time. I go to the studio operations desk, where I am fitted with a Lavaliere microphone and an earpiece. The microphone is small and gets clipped to my shirt. The wire runs underneath my shirt to the transmitter that gets clipped to the back of my pants. The earpiece also runs through my shirt and is attached to a second unit. I look at a large box full of batteries below me. I'm told they go through millions of batteries a year. After a certain amount of hours, they toss them into a giant box, whether they're still good or not. They have to change them well before they fail.

The person preparing my electronics presses a button under the counter, "I have Nick on line 3." In a moment I hear a voice over my earpiece, "Go ahead Nick on 3." I count to 10. "That's great," I hear the voice again in my earpiece. I'm moments away from going on air.

I make my way to the set. As I stand at my demonstration table, I see the host in the monitors in front of me. The time is counting down in the left monitor. From my earlier meeting with the coordinating producer, I know where my product is slotted. By the time I'm on the set and ready to go, I might be two products away from my segment.

I've been here many times before, so I'm not really nervous. Anxious usually, because you never know what can happen. It might be the last time your product is on, or you might be very successful. It's all very unpredictable, but once you have done your best in preparation, it's more or less out of your hands, so I try to relax.

I check over my demonstration to make sure I have everything in place one final time. The host arrives. The handheld camera operator stands off to the side. Then I am introduced, and we're off—the overview of the product . . . the demo . . . the testimonial caller . . . another demo . . . and blip, we're done. "Thanks for coming," the host says, and off he or she goes to the next set.

I break down my set and head off to the green room to see how I've done.

The car rides home from QVC have mostly been good ones, and I count my blessings every time I get a chance to make more money in six minutes than most people make in a year. There is a lot of preparation that goes into those six minutes, and I never forget my beginnings. It's a well-earned living, and it's an amazing opportunity.

I'm always amazed at people's stories that are just like mine. I love to hear about how they came up with their ideas and the path they took to get to QVC, how we all have the same thing in common of how suddenly, as if from nowhere, we were afforded the opportunity to reach millions of people.

As I drive home, I think about these things, and I'm always grateful that I met the right people at the right time and made the right moves. I'm grateful that I was fortunate enough to create fantastic products that help many people do the things they love. I'm proof that anyone can do it.

12

The Two Most Important Words You Can Associate with Your Product

The two most important words you can hear at QVC are *sold out.* It means that everything you worked for has come to fruition. It means that everything you manufactured and shipped has been sold. It means your buyers were successful. It means everyone you hoped would love your product is now going to be receiving and benefiting from it. And it means you will undoubtedly be returning to QVC.

This simple little phrase leaves you with a success story for your next appearance. It's the best testimonial when it comes to social proof. You offered a product, and everyone loved it. Getting a sellout means you made it over first-appearance jitters. It ripples through your entire business, and you can now not only claim, "As seen on TV," for your product, but you can also tell prospective retail buyers that your product sold out on QVC. It validates your business, your product, and all your efforts to the outside world.

But what if you didn't sell out—were you still successful? This is one of the most difficult questions to answer. Ask ten knowledgeable people in the QVC world, and you will get ten different answers. The answer is known by the "invisible people" at QVC, the *unreachables,* as some people call them. I'm referring to the QVC planners.

All kidding aside, the answer to the question of whether you were successful is, "It depends." It depends on the hour of the day that you were on. It depends on the day of the week you were on. It depends on your product category, the type of segment you appeared on, or if you were part of a special full-day event. The time of year you were on also plays a factor in interpreting your on-air numbers. It really varies according to these and other variables. As the market environment changes, so do the benchmarks.

I've been asked to return to QVC after selling as low as $4,000 per minute. This is in retail dollars, and it translates to the total retail sales (the price to the consumer times the number of units sold) divided by the amount of time in the on-air segment. It is a common way of looking at performance.

So, for example, if you had 3,000 units in stock and their retail price each is $20, and you sold 2,000 units in six minutes, your sales per minute would be: 2,000 units $\times$ $20 each = $40,000 $\rightarrow$ $40,000/6 minutes = $6,667 per minute.

I've been told by agents and buyers that over $6,000 per minute is good for daytime airings that have a guest, and over $2,000 per minute is acceptable for overnight airings. Again, this changes.

My experience has varied. Sometimes the whole hour I've appeared on performs below par. Maybe it was the weather, or a world event, or time of day. More than a few times I've performed so poorly, along with everyone else in the same hour, that someone in planning must have declared a "mulligan," because we got a "do-over" and were able to redeem ourselves with a second chance. From a vendor standpoint, it seems it's not always science, and there is room for interpretation.

In aviation, they say that any landing you can walk away from is a good landing. It doesn't matter if you came in on one wheel or grinded your propeller in the pavement: If you are alive when your wheels come to a halt at the end of the runway, you performed a great landing. Although the same philosophy applied to QVC might seem a cop-out, in the end, the best way to gauge whether you were successful is whether you get invited back.

CHAPTER 13

Getting Paid, Returns, Backorders, and Surges

Getting Paid

Although any terms of your relationship with QVC are negotiable, standard practice, based on my experience, is that you will receive payment within 30 days after your on-air appearance for the amount of goods sold (your price to QVC) less any deductions for damaged or returned merchandise. (This information is included in the purchase order.)

I have heard of other home shopping channels that do not pay within a reasonable time, but my experience with QVC in regard to receiving timely payments has been extremely good. In fact, after my largest sales effort, I received a reorder for the same item before I was scheduled to get paid for the first order. I had really gone out on a limb to finance the manufacturing of the 22,080 units called for on the original order, and my resources were depleted. After sharing this with my buyer, she arranged payment in full, and within a week I was back in business.

QVC's outlook is a pleasant departure from my experiences with other mass merchants such as chain stores. Not all, but many mass merchants think that stretching a vendor's payment to 180 days or more is good for their business.

It might be good for their cash flow and their interest-gaining investment vehicles and financial statements, but it doesn't make me rush to do business with them. It does, however, give me another strong reason why I'm a big proponent of doing business with QVC.

Returns

Returns come in two forms. The first kind is *customer returns.* These are when a customer purchases the item from QVC and decides to exercise QVC's thirty-day return policy. The customer may have changed his or her mind; the product might not be what was expected, and so on.

QVC has a reasonable return policy for its customers, and customer returns are an everyday part of doing business with QVC as a vendor. The returns are generally accumulated by the QVC warehouse and shipped to you in quantity, so you won't necessarily be receiving one return at a time.

If you inspect the returns, you will discover a variety of findings. Sometimes the return is an unopened box, sometimes it is has been used, and sometimes it comes back with missing pieces.

In any event, expect to get returns anywhere between 2 and 5 percent of the quantity sold, unless you have an agreement where QVC absorbs the returns.

The other kind of return is the dreaded *return to vendor,* or RTV. RTVs occur for several reasons. One example that will trigger a RTV is if you ship your product to QVC and it is not as specified according to the quality assurance sample you first submitted. When the delivery is made at the warehouse, the receiving department will inspect it by taking a random sampling of the items in the shipment and compare their findings to what is in their database. If there is a problem, they may call for a RTV.

Other times when you'll receive an RTV notice is if your product is unsuccessful or when it nears the end of its run.

A word of encouragement: Not being successful on QVC doesn't always mean your product is not going to be successful elsewhere. As I've said before, the television shopping industry on the whole is very unpredictable. I have seen many products thought to have the greatest potential for QVC's style and audience do miserably with no substantiation. Some QVC failures go on to sell extremely well in stores, catalogs, and online, so it's not always an accurate barometer for success.

If you're a thriving business, returns might not be a big deal for you. However, if you're a small business, they can really hurt you. When my company was a fledgling business I would develop a product with an exit strategy in mind. Meaning, I felt it important to know what to do with our product if we didn't sell all of it on TV. We were doing a lot of consumer trade shows at the time, and so I only developed product that I could bundle properly for television AND that fit our formula for selling on the road.

There are many other options for selling returned and unsold items, and careful planning can help make the transition smooth. A short list could include any number of Internet options, such as eBay, your own Web site, and craigslist. (Check out www.SellonQ. com and click on Free Resources.) If you sell to stores, consider creating product for QVC that can easily be repackaged for retail.

Other possibilities include selling to companies in search of overstocked items that they purchase in bulk and then resell through their outlets. The most obvious mainstream example is the Web site overstock.com. Depending on your product and its viability for appealing to the masses, you might have to do a little bit of digging to uncover a company that is right for you.

Getting returns is a cost of doing business, and it gets trickier as your product's life cycle nears its end and you stand a chance of getting thousands of units back in one shipment if you're not careful.

My advice would be to track your sales and communicate with your buyer. If you're putting together a string of poor performances and you have low inventory or perhaps you just sold out the remainder of your inventory, consider putting an end to the product. If the product has been successful, this might be a good time to reinvent it and/or develop a deluxe version that you can bring back to QVC. Our Kreate-a-lopes® have been through five successful reconfigurations to date, and we've been able to minimize returns at the end of each life cycle by studying our sales figures.

On a side note, you might be wondering what happens to unsold merchandise that QVC doesn't return to you. For one, it has five outlets that are filled with great bargains. For another, it partners with established wholesalers, retailers, and exporters to sell off inventory that is no longer sold on air. This includes close-outs, first-quality goods, quality rejects, second-quality goods, and customer returns.

If you're a go-getter entrepreneur, this might be a viable source of quality merchandise that you can acquire at or below wholesale cost. Visit www.SellonQ.com/Q-outlets for more information about these locations.

Backorders and Surges

Good news. You sold out, you're done demonstrating, and QVC continued to take orders. If this happens, you will receive a *backorder.* Backorders are generally small orders, and in my experience I have always been given plenty of time to fill them. I have even been in a position where we had zero inventory in our factory and had to wait until our next production run to capture economies of scale, which means a longer-than-usual turnaround time.

The other type of backorder that I have only a little experience with is referred to as a *surge.* This happens when producers decide to keep you on-air well beyond the time you have sold out of inventory. The qualifier is, they will ask you if you have the ability to ship the more-than-usual backorder immediately.

14

How to Add Easy Money to Your Bottom Line, and Other Ways to Drive Your Success

Whene businesses are trying to increase sales, it has been said that one of the most overlooked prospects is their existing customer base. If this is true, then why not sell to your existing customers?

Thinking along similar lines, consider the effort it takes to motivate a television viewer to pick up the telephone and order your product. In essence, this person is a customer, albeit one that has not yet used and experienced the benefits of your product. But even so, this soon-to-be customer has already turned the corner to becoming a believer and is likely to buy more from you.

The Upsell

You may have heard of the term *upsell* before. If you haven't and you watch television, I know you've seen this sales technique in action. It's a very powerful sales tool that has consistently added 20 to 40 percent in revenue to our bottom line. In short, it's a way of selling more to people that have warmed up to your product and have already made the decision to buy from you.

As it relates to QVC, an upsell is a complementary product that is offered to buyers while they are on the telephone purchasing the main item. Here is how it works. The viewer sees the product being demonstrated QVC and calls the toll-free number to place an order.

After the QVC customer service representative has taken the order, the representative offers the caller the upsell product, if there is one available. The representative never uses the term *upsell*—rather, it is simply offered to the customer as an additional item being made available to them.

The upsell is most effective when it is closely related to the main product, and has a much lower price point. Perhaps the primary product is a set of knives for $25. The upsell product could be a knife sharpener for $15.

Outside of QVC, an upsell is often defined as an upgrade. One example of this is an offer in the buying process to go from a silver to a gold membership.

In business, there are generally three ways you can increase the revenue to your company:

1. Increase the exposure of your product(s).
2. Increase the revenue per sale.
3. Sell additional products to your existing customer base after they become a customer.

The upsell falls into #2 and can arguably fall into #3, as well.

In my experience, 20 percent of the people who have purchased our primary product have also purchased the upsell product when we have offered one. Our highest has been around 40 percent. Imagine selling 10,000 units of your primary item and 2,000 to 4,000 additional units of a second item simply by adding it to your offering.

This little extra effort has generated hundreds upon hundreds of thousands of dollars for us, and it's easy to do. Simply create an accessory or complementary product to your primary product that you can offer at a reduced price and present it to your buyers when you pitch your primary product. If it is deemed of value to the consumers in the eyes of QVC and they add it to the offering, you're on your way to more profits.

Be forewarned that ultimately, you should be creating a product of true value and use to the customers. If you betray their trust, they may never order any of your products again.

The close neighbor to this style of upsell that you are likely more familiar with is the one you see on television infomercials that goes something like this: "And if you call now, you'll get our deluxe knife sharpener for free. . . ."

This type of upsell was first used by Ron Popeil and his contemporaries in the early days of television and is not used by QVC.

As of this writing, QVC limits its upsells to one additional product. Infomercials, by contrast, might announce one or two bonus offerings for customers placing the order immediately, and once you get on the phone they may have as many as a dozen additional products. You might be responding to a $19.95 offer and walk away with a bill four times what you expected to pay for your Deluxe Kitchen Mop because you bought a bundle of accessories!

A great example of upselling in today's marketplace is Amazon. com. It has countless upsells integrated into its selling process, right along with upsell's close cousin, the *cross-sell*, which is akin to buying a book by John Steinbeck and being offered another by Mark Twain before you checkout. It's not directly related but might be of similar interest.

The Adapted Loss Leader

We've used a strategy based on the concept of a *loss leader* and although it's not a primary strategy, it has proven to be advantageous to us under certain circumstances.

A *loss leader*, by marketing definitions, is a type of pricing strategy where an item is sold below cost in an effort to stimulate other profitable sales.

A typical loss leader is an item offered by a store at such a low price that the store is losing money on the item with every sale. The store knows that the typical customer will purchase other items at the same time as they are purchasing the loss leader and that the profit made on these other items will generate an overall profit for the store.

In today's competitive marketplace, it is sometimes difficult for a company placing a small order for materials to compete with a company placing a large order for similar material. The larger orders benefit by what is referred to as *economies of scale,* which means that, up to a certain point, per-unit costs drop as the number of units produced or shipped increases. Thus, buyers of large orders will get a lower price per unit than buyers of small orders. This translates to higher profit margins if your selling price remains the same. It also affords you the ability to drop your selling price and remain profitable while providing a better value to the customer. In a competitive environment, however, this generates a baseline price for certain items. When this happens, stores, or—in our case—QVC, comes to expect to pay only a certain price for an item based on previous experience. In other words, if you try to sell QVC paper at $0.25 per sheet, when it has been paying half that amount from other vendors, you'll have to justify your price difference. However, if you are the only one producing a unique fabric being used in clothing, then your pricing is more determined by your costs and market perception.

So, in light of baseline price awareness, under certain circumstances we've approached our pricing strategy using the essence of the loss leader. For example, we know that we must remain competitively priced with our primary item. If we need to place small orders for material, we can't benefit from economies of scale. But since there is a baseline price awareness, we can't just bump up our price and expect to get a purchase order. So, we bring our primary item to QVC at the great price it has come to expect and then also create an upsell item that affords us the opportunity to price it fairly to the customer, yet at a slightly higher margin to help us compensate for the lower margin on the first item.

Additionally, we might use this strategy when we want to affect a lower retail price even when we are benefiting from economies of scale to begin with. For example, after developing an item, we find that at our normal margin, and after QVC adds its margin, the item will sell for a retail price of $31. We know that the item would sell better if it had a retail of $29, so we drop our price in order to reach this number.

Then we develop an upsell product and build in a slightly higher percentage than our regular margin. We don't increase the cost of the upsell item by $2 to compensate for the $2 differential with the primary product in this example, but we add a small percentage.

Now, we're not guaranteed that QVC will accept the upsell, nor are we guaranteed that the buyers will accept our selling price for it, but if they do, we can make up some of our lost profit from the lower price of the primary item.

It's difficult to measure, but if you're able to generate more sales by lowering the price of your primary product, then more people will be offered the upsell, and if 20 to 30 percent of those additional people purchase the upsell, you will increase your revenues and exposure to your product on the whole.

Building Momentum

Extrapolating the possibilities even further, consider how important a sellout on QVC would be for you. A sellout likely means that you will be invited back. A sellout might also mean that you'll move from an overnight test spot, if that's where you started, to a primetime airing, where you can quadruple your sales. Reaching this goal might just be the catalyst for building the forward momentum that will catapult sales for your company both on and outside of QVC.

In my coaching group, I often ask the question, "Are you willing to sell your product at cost if it means you will get in the door and potentially build a lifelong relationship with QVC, where you will be able to sell more products in the future at regular margins?"

The question might seem ridiculous to some, but it supports the often-professed strategy of many marketers to "sacrifice early profits" in order to gain momentum and product awareness.

This is essentially what King Gillette did with his razor at the turn of the last century. In the late 1890s, there weren't many alternatives to how you shaved your face. You either used a straight razor or you didn't shave. It was a nuisance, and shaving with a straight razor was a difficult, painful, and dangerous task.

Gillette was a traveling salesman at the time. The president of the company that employed him was William Painter, who was also the inventor of an improved bottle stopper. It was a crimped bottle cap that became the standard of the day in the bottling industry.

Painter and Gillette were also friends. They shared a kindred inventor's spirit. In their many conversations, Painter encouraged

Gillette to invent something that could be used and thrown away. This became an obsession for Gillette, until one morning while shaving, he had a flash of inspiration for a disposable razor.

Yet experts of the day told Gillette that it was impossible to produce steel hard enough and thin enough, yet cheap enough, to make the razor blades disposable. Faced with these limitations however, he persevered, and in 1904 received a patent for his invention. He went on to price his razors dirt cheap, knowing that if he could get men to try it, they would come back to him forever for the razor blades.

It was a runaway success. In his second year of business, his company produced 90,000 razors and 12,400,000 blades. Years later, during the first World War, Gillette's razor was given to every soldier, alongside weapons and uniforms. This created a base of future customers that would continue buying razors long after their time in the military.

Gillette understood that by sacrificing early profits he would be able to position himself for a lifetime of loyal customers. Using this mentality can also create a lifelong customer base with your product at QVC. For this reason, careful consideration should be given to the product offered, pricing, and upsell offers.

Promoting Your Appearance

So, what can you do to ensure a sellout on QVC? Should you drop your price? Should you add incredible value to your offering? In truth, these things should be considered, but doing so will still not guarantee a sellout. The landscape is simply too unpredictable. However, it is prudent marketing to leave no opportunities behind. This includes promoting your upcoming appearance on QVC to the outside world.

One way you can do this is by advertising. You might be asking, "Why? Isn't that the point of being on television? Won't I be advertising the advertisement?" The point is that you want to consider all opportunities for being a success on QVC. By weighing the concept of sacrificing early profits, you can create a demand for your product, a lifetime customer by way of the viewer, and a lifelong customer in QVC by being successful.

What might a second, third, or more appearances mean for your product, not to mention the residual sales you might realize in your regular business as a result of advertising in the first place? You might be thinking that you're paying for advertising and losing profits, but you might be gaining that back in volume and consumer awareness. Think of the grocery stores that operate at 5 to 6 percent margins but realize profits by selling in mass quantity. By spreading the word to the outside world, you're essentially doubling your exposure for potential profit. In the end, each situation has its own set of circumstances, and how and why you promote will have to be closely evaluated.

Momentum is critical to the launch of any product. On the one hand, it's often experienced; on the other hand, it's difficult to quantify and pinpoint. Simply examine the importance of momentum in realizing your product's acceptance by the masses and what will happen once you hit what is commonly referred to as the *tipping point*. By increasing your exposure through advertising, which, in turn, might promote word-of-mouth marketing and general customer awareness, you are possibly getting the jump start you need to succeed on television.

In Internet marketing, we have at our fingertips the ability to measure this momentum by using what is called a tell-a-friend script. A basic tell-a-friend script contains a button near an article or product. When and if visitors click on the button, they can send the information to a friend.

Although the basic tell-a-friend script has lost its effectiveness, a modified tell-a-friend script with a bonus feature attached has not, and can be used as an example of how quickly word of mouth can spread for something new and exciting.

A tell-a-friend script with a bonus attached basically works like this: A visitor sees your product or article and is offered an incentive to spread the word. Often, it is a free gift, coupon, or download of some kind. Most scripts allow you to change the number of friends that are required in order to get the bonus. Setting this number to three, for example, increases the viral nature of your marketing efforts because in order to qualify for the bonus, three friends' names and e-mails will have to be entered in the form.

Now, thanks to the power of the Internet, where everything can and should be measured, you can see how quickly things of this nature work or fail. It is not uncommon for us to set up a tell-a-friend with a bonus, send the offer to 100 people, and see the number of participants jump geometrically to 1,000 in as little as an hour. Increase the first notification to 15,000, and the viral spread of the message reaches larger numbers even faster. The point is, even though you can't see or pinpoint the effect of momentum in traditional forms of advertising, it exists.

We've made available a list of free resources for readers of this book that contains information on tell-a-friend scripts, Web design, development, hosting, Internet marketing, and more. It can be found by visiting www.SellonQ.com and clicking on Free Resources.

Use Your Web Site for Maximum Benefit

Short and sweet, make sure you have a Web site and make sure its address is on your product label, if possible. I mentioned in Chapter 9 how QVC rejects most bouncebacks. Having your Web site listed alongside your regular company information is not a bounceback. Only when you attempt to solicit customers through your wording will it raise flags with QVC's quality assurance and legal departments. Add your Web site with no solicitations. If people like your product, they will likely visit your Web site or refer others to it long after they forgot where they found you in the first place.

More importantly though, is that by having a Web site, you will likely realize sales from and around your QVC appearance. I have been dumbfounded by this from the very beginning. Why would someone watch a product on television, want it, and then shy away from the much-respected source that introduced it to them—QVC—only to go search for the item on the Internet? I don't know why—maybe they're disgruntled, maybe they think they're going to get a better deal—I'm perplexed as to the reason it happens but it does, and sometimes in large numbers.

This is an added plus for us, because we sell at full retail on our Web site. Many of our margins are as high as 70 percent for our products because we manufacture them ourselves. If you manufacture

your own products and also sell direct to the public, you might realize the same margins. So, make sure you have a Web site, and better
yet, make sure you show up in the search engines for any terms you
will be queried for, such as product name, product type, company
name, or product category. Search engine optimization is beyond
the scope of this book, but there are plenty of companies that can
assist you in gaining a searchable presence on the Internet.

Lastly, if you've been on the Internet for a while and/or have
access to lists of people who have either purchased from you in the
past or have an interest in your category, you can send them a notice
about your upcoming appearance on QVC. One of my colleagues
was scheduled for QVC's Today's Special Value and blasted her enor-
mous list prior to her show. She presold 15,000 units.

15

Six Mistakes that Can Snap the Back of Your Business, and How to Avoid Them

Costly Mistake to Avoid #1

I watched a story on one of the news journal shows recently about a man who had created a dental hygiene product and hoped to get a purchase order from QVC or HSN.

As the host and the man walked in a warehouse full of his *one* product, the man explained that he had manufactured it ahead of time and was ready to sell it on a home shopping show. The problem was, he did not have a firm order from any channel. There it was for all to see—his product, stacked high in the rented warehouse with nowhere to go.

I was amazed to hear that the man had mortgaged his home to produce the inventory they were showing us. My recollection is that it cost him somewhere in the neighborhood of $850,000 to manufacture this yet unsold, uncontracted for, product.

I saw a man with a vision, an invention, a sizable mortgage, and only a wish that one of the major home shopping shows would take him on. It's not like he already had a relationship with QVC or HSN that he was going to parlay into an order for this new item. He had nothing. And the TV crew was there to film it.

I laugh, because I have manufactured product in my own past before I had a single firm order. And even though I had produced product (on a smaller scale than that of the man on the news program) with the intention of selling it directly to stores, it was and still is a potentially costly mistake to avoid.

Here is the bottom line, whether you intend on selling to stores or to one of the major home shopping shows. Build a prototype—an accurate working model of the yet-to-be produced product. If it comes in a kit, create the components that go in the kit, along with the proposed packaging.

Use the prototype to sell your idea and secure a purchase order. At the very least you should be able to secure a purchase order "contingent upon approval of a production quality finished sample." Along with this, communicate your lead time for manufacturing (days needed to produce the product) in advance.

The two glaring risks that the man in the news program had taken were that he did not yet have an order, and if he did get an order, the customer might want him to make a change. QVC, for example, might require that any number of things be changed, ranging from quality assurance issues to package wording to contents of the product. Rework is expensive, and manufacturing any quantity of product before you have an order is one of the quickest ways to get into financial trouble. Needless to say, these two situations should be avoided at all costs.

Costly Mistake to Avoid #2

Every product has a life cycle. Introducing a new and improved version of the product before the life cycle of the original product has run its course can cost you a lot in lost profits, lost time, and the new and improved version might not be as successful as the original.

Several years ago, there was a small company selling a craft item on QVC. It was a unique little product that had compiled a string of sellouts. We all watched in amazement as, show after show, the product sold out. It was such a runaway success that the company owners were invited on one of the major daytime talk shows for a segment about millionaires.

Then, without warning, the product disappeared from any of the regularly scheduled craft days, only to appear months later with a new and improved version.

The owners missed the first warning sign. The product was selling, and selling well, so there was no reason to change it. Another warning sign: In order to manufacture the item, a specialized injection molded component was required. I was told by the woman and her inventor husband that the tooling for the new and improved item cost over $100,000 to create.

You might think this is a high cost, but from their vantage point at the time, it's understandable why they made the decision to forge ahead. They were selling out like crazy and they saw no end in sight, so why not make a bigger and better version?

The costly lesson here, though, is about ending a successful product's life cycle before it matures. At QVC, especially at the time this particular product was on-air, many products could make a two-, maybe three-year run. By cutting their product short, they clearly lost any future opportunities to appear on any television show spotlighting millionaires.

The other costly mistake made on their part was due to inexperience. These individuals had come to QVC on their own gumption, unrepresented. Possibly, they were discovered by QVC during one of their open calls or at a trade show. I remember asking them in the green room why they spent all the money on the re-tooling and introducing the new version, and their response was that their buyer at QVC told them they should to do it.

It was a big mistake that anyone can see in hindsight, but only someone with experience would have been able to avoid it as it was unfolding. I'm not saying the QVC buyer didn't have the experience. What I am saying is, had they had an agent, or consulted with one, or anyone, for that matter, with a lot of real-world QVC experience, they would have been able to make a stronger case for sticking with the runaway hit that their original version was.

My agent and I talked about this particular case at length many times, especially when we were faced with our own decisions about when and what changes to implement to our existing product line.

In an earlier chapter I mentioned how good agents usually pay for themselves by knowing how to price a product and by being able to secure more airings by being knowledgeable. Well, this is another reason to have an agent if you can. A good one simply knows what to do and when to do it and can save you a lot of money in mistakes.

Costly Mistake to Avoid #3

I found a dynamic product with a charismatic demonstrator one time at a major craft and hobby trade show. It was the perfect product for QVC, and everything about the presentation spelled success. "Tom" was energetic, the product was unusual yet mainstream for the category, and the demonstration could be completed fairly quickly with a "wow" of a result.

I visited the booth several times during the trade show, and each time there was a large, excited group of people watching. Tom, the inventor of the product, dazzled everyone with his innovation.

At the end of the trade show, my hunch about the product was proven correct when Tom's small company took home the most innovative product award. Fortunately for us, my agent and I had already spoken to him about presenting his product to QVC and had a handshake agreement to move forward on his behalf.

Fast forward four months to the QVC set. I had been busy with my own setups and last-minute details. My agent was back and forth, assisting several new clients and speaking to producers about camera angles, times, and the like, so we didn't get much of a chance to communicate. I had already been at QVC for a number of years and needed very little in the way of technical guidance, so not getting a chance to speak with him was not unusual.

Suddenly Tom was next to my table. This was the first I'd seen him since introducing him to my agent at the trade show. Big grins came across our faces. It was a huge achievement to be where we were, and now Tom was experiencing what I first described to him at the trade show four months prior.

In my grin, there was a brotherly joy, too. I knew what could happen from this point forward, and I was happy to be a big part of his travels. But Tom's grin filled the room. It was a first timer's grin. It was the grin of a man standing at the pinnacle of product exposure, moments away from *the ten-minute rush* that could do more for his company than five years of trade shows.

"So, are you ready?" I asked him.

"Yeah." He responded enthusiastically.

"When are you going on?" I asked.

"Oh, my wife's over there, she's going on."

Screech! My brain came to a sudden halt. *"What?"* I stuttered, confused.

"Yeah, we thought it was the right thing to have a woman demonstrating, being a crafting item and all."

From that point forward every contract we ever put in front of anyone contained the clause, "We reserve the right to determine and approve the on-air personality selected to demonstrate the product."

In all the time I spent in Tom's booth at the trade show, I never once saw his wife demonstrate the product. It was his energy that rocked the house, and with their decision to have his wife demonstrate, Tom had made a costly mistake.

No offense to his wife, but Tom was a born communicator. Years of dealing with people in his normal job and years of being a fun-loving, vibrant man with a lot to offer the world had made him the perfect on-air guest. It was because of him that we knew the product would be a hit. It was his charisma that pushed his invention into the limelight with a most innovative trophy at the largest trade show in our industry.

On top of that, what Tom didn't realize was something I knew from the first time I had ever demonstrated my product to a room full of craft enthusiasts— a room full of women that filled my classroom a hundred strong because the only man in the whole place was there and about to demonstrate a new craft item. Tom missed the mark—the women in crafting love, love, love to see a vibrant man demonstrating a craft item to them.

In the blur of mental confusion that followed Tom's announcement to me, I tried to convince him that he should be the one to demonstrate, but his mind was set. My big brotherly grin had faded, and that would be the last time I would see Tom on the QVC set. His wife was lifeless in front of the camera, and so were their sales.

This costly mistake could have been avoided by selecting the best demonstrator for the product. Sometimes it's the inventor and sometimes it isn't. Sometimes egos are a problem in making the best choice. Maybe the owner of the company wants the spotlight. Maybe someone wants his girlfriend to be the one, and the only one that sees the reason is the honcho calling the shots.

A successful demonstrator can be anyone. Sometimes the best demonstrators have no experience. Sometimes they're your chatty neighbor. People don't need to have sales, trade show, or any public speaking experience to be good. It helps, but you just have to know. If you don't know or feel biased, find someone that can advise you or get multiple opinions and pick the best.

Costly Mistake to Avoid #4

This one goes out to all the small business owners. If you're a one-man show like I was in the beginning, you need to read this section.

Without belaboring the point, don't rush through the manufacturing process of your product just to make a deadline. You will get your chance if you need to take more time to manufacture your product, but if you make a mistake because you rushed the manufacturing process you might never get another chance.

We had received a purchase order for a box-making kit we had developed. It contained a slick little template that was extremely versatile. It showed crafters how to make a myriad of boxes from pillow boxes to pyramid boxes to rectangular and square boxes. The product was not easy or cheap to make. It called for injection molding, and the tooling cost exceeded twenty thousand dollars. I had also invested a considerable amount of time developing the product, so there was a lot more than money at stake.

I was under a shipping deadline with QVC, and to complicate matters, I had scheduled a business trip to England, which further compressed my timeline. The end result was that I hastily approved the final mold.

On the day of the flight overseas, a bizarre turn of events caused me to cancel the trip. This gave me time to go to the manufacturing facility. Standing on the factory floor, minutes before commencing the run for nearly ten thousand units, I noticed something in the template that was about to be molded. Upon closer inspection, I realized a major oversight. We stopped the production, I indicated the change to be made, and the mold was corrected.

In my haste I could have shipped a defective product that would have cost a bundle to recall, not to mention the negative impact it would have had with my still-new relationship with QVC. Fortunately, I saved myself from what would have been a crippling hit to my fledgling business and avoided a costly mistake.

Take your time, do it right, and double-check your work—every bit of it.

Costly Mistake to Avoid #5

If you sell on QVC, don't sell on HSN, the Home Shopping Network. HSN is second to QVC in terms of home shopping show sales, and if you try to sell on both stations concurrently, QVC will likely stop ordering from you.

Based on what I've seen and heard, this relates more to the guest that appears on-air for the given product line. If you consider the affiliation that is made between the expert demonstrator and an item, it is understandable why a network would not want a company to do both channels simultaneously. It dilutes the value of the guest and the exclusive nature of the product offering.

For this same reason, QVC also allows demonstrators to demonstrate products in only one category. The exception is if a period of six months has passed from the previous demonstration. This is because having an on-air guest personality demonstrate crafts one day, then fashion the next, dilutes the demonstrator's perceived expert status in either category.

The bottom line: Avoid the costly mistake of losing either station as a customer by trying to sell on both simultaneously.

Costly Mistake to Avoid #6

The goal: Preserve your success and avoid bad airtimes. The problem: You can't control airtime, but you can influence it.

Imagine, for example, that you have been asked to go on-air with your sun visor product on December 1st. Your company data shows that summer is your best sales season for this particular product and December is dismal for your product no matter what the sales venue. Now, I don't sell sun visor products, and this scenario might seem outlandish to some, but similar things have happened to me whether they involved mismatched seasons, mismatched segments, or awful dates for selling our products like December 22. The question is, what do you do?

New vendors often have to take what is given them. On one hand, if you have a dismal first appearance, it's a slim chance that you'll return. On the other hand, if you have compiled a string of successes and you have one dismal appearance, it will likely not affect QVC's decision to bring you back. However, put together two or three poor performances, and you're on your way out the door.

I can't speak for QVC or how programmers make their decisions, but sometimes I think they need to fill a slot and your product comes up. Many buyers will understand your position if you present it to them in light of your recent performance(s), just as they will sometimes give you a low quantity order so your chances of achieving a sellout increase and your product will be easier to position for the next sell.

If you think the proposed airdate is not conducive to your success, sometimes getting it changed is as simple as reminding the buyer of your product's strengths. Circumstances revolving around your availability as well as your ability to manufacture product can also influence airdates. For example, if you have inventory in QVC's warehouse and you receive a request for what you believe to be a less-than-desirable airdate, that's one thing. However, if you have to manufacture and ship product in order for QVC to have enough inventory for the given on-air appearance and you can't make the deadline for whatever reason, you won't be scheduled.

I'm not advising to mislead anyone, but if you can't ship product, or if you are unavailable as an on-air guest because you have a scheduled business trip, you will not be added to the lineup.

Lastly, another way to receive better air times is to enlist the services of a marquee guest personality. This is a person in your category who has an established track record of success. When this occurs two things usually happen—the person attracts a lot of viewers, and, by virtue of their success, they are often scheduled regularly. Sometimes, shows are created specifically for the person as well.

Working with a marquee personality might involve licensing your product to the company they represent, bringing the product in through their agent, or in some cases, hiring them straightaway to do your demonstration. If your product fits into segments that the marquee personality appears on regularly, it may be included in the lineup.

CHAPTER 16

Open Doors to Greater Success

One appearance on QVC can open many doors for you. Being able to add an *As Seen on TV* logo to your product packaging or using your appearance to add credibility to your company is invaluable. This chapter will show you many ways to leverage and make the most out of even just one appearance on the home shopping giant.

Retail Stores

I did not know a thing about the retail side of the business when I first came to QVC. My retail education was limited to seeing products in the local store and taking a wild guess at the markup and how the process worked.

I didn't know how to create packaging or how to sell to stores, I knew pretty much nothing. But it didn't stop me from sending a plain letter (without even a colorful catalog sheet) to a handful of small stores and one major chain store buyer to announce my first appearance on QVC. The truth is, when I look at the letter today I laugh and ask myself, "What was I thinking?"

The result, however, proved to be well worth my efforts, as I received two orders from small stores and an order for 25,000 units from the only major chain I sent my letter to. If my first QVC appearance was a one-time thing because I didn't do well, it would have still been a success based on what I did outside of QVC. Fortunately, I had success with both.

The other thing to consider is, not only did I receive initial orders from stores, but from that point forward the orders became a continuous stream. I can easily make a case for the massive ripple effect my first appearance on QVC created—it would fill up this book. For that reason, I strongly recommend that you add a mailing to stores or potential customers to your preshow marketing list once you know your air date. It could pay large dividends.

Networking and Co-ventures

I always tell my friends that you never know what's on the other side of the door until you walk in. Your whole life might change. You might see something you never saw before. You might meet people you might never have met otherwise. I believe trusting in oneself is part of the process even if you can't foresee what might be ahead of you. Being open has been a key to many doors that have positively affected the growth of my business.

When you make it to QVC, one thing that you'll find for sure is other people much like yourself. You will also find people who are much higher on the ladder of success. Being part of QVC is like being part of an elite club and the default meeting area is the green room. It is a mecca for meeting other successful business owners that may become friends or future co-venture partners.

I made many friends and created many co-ventures as a result of my experience with QVC. One of the most significant for my business included a co-venture with a major company that put us into 22,000 stores in twenty-three countries.

The experience not only gave our product exposure and added revenue to our financials but also opened more doors for other co-ventures. In addition, it added more credibility to our small company. This would never have happened had I not befriended the CEO of this company and spent many business and social hours together—and it all started in the QVC green room.

Another door that opened after getting to QVC was the interest of other companies to acquire us. The most notable offer came from a $40 million company in our industry. And while I turned down its eventual offer to acquire all my patents and my entire business, it was a valuable experience that validated our direction as a company.

The experience also sharpened my business acumen and taught me the value and reason some large companies want to acquire smaller companies—to expand their product lines and gain a larger customer base.

QVC United Kingdom and QVC Germany

Another door that opened for us once we were successful on QVC in the United States was that of QVC United Kingdom and QVC Germany. Buyers in London and Duesseldorf contacted my agent, and once we showed interest, they requested samples of our products. Purchase orders and proposed airdates followed soon after. (Although QVC also broadcasts in Japan, as of this writing I do not have any experience there.)

My experiences in England and Germany have all been well received and very positive for us as a business. And they've been fun, too. The first time I went to England, I brought my wife and we took time to see the sights. Upon arriving at Buckingham Palace, playing tourists, there was a big rush of people to the gates, which is where we happened to be. As we looked around we suddenly realized that everyone wanted to be where we were standing. Not knowing what was going on, but knowing that we had coveted real estate, we stood firm and watched attentively—for what, we didn't know, but it felt important.

Moments later, guards threw open the gates and an entourage of expensive cars started streaming in. Cameras began flashing, people were pushing and screaming, and there we were with our noses pressed against the gates peering between the bars. As the third car passed, I spotted Prince Charles sitting in the back, expressionless. He was the only recognizable face I saw in the dozen cars that entered the palace, but apparently it was enough to cause people to get giddy over the experience. And that was only the beginning for us on this trip.

About an hour later, as we made our way toward another tourist hotspot, Big Ben, my wife and I saw a lot of people gathering in the blocks ahead of us. We also noticed that the police were in full force. When we got to the street with all the commotion, we couldn't tell what was going on so we continued on our way. But just as we stepped off the curb to cross the street, a big bobby, as their police are called, dropped a blue wooden barricade in front of us and nearly squashed my foot.

Again, just like at Buckingham Palace, people started screaming and cameras started flashing, and we had a prime location. I thought to myself, is Prince Charles driving around again? But then I asked the bobby what was going on and he proudly stated that Her Majesty the Queen was coming through.

I looked down the street, and sure enough, I saw her. She was in a massive car and was wearing a red hat. I could see her very well because there was a light on in the car that highlighted her for the adoration of her subjects. Once again, we were in the front row witnessing England's royalty.

Later that night, when we arrived at QVC studios on Queensboro Road, one of the locals in the green room asked me if we had had a chance to see London. I told him about seeing Prince Charles and the Queen. In minutes everyone in the room was gathering around me to hear the story. And some were touching me as if I was some kind of lucky-charmed Leprechaun. One of them told us that people live in England their whole lives and never see the Royal Family, and we were incredibly lucky to see two of them in one day.

I think about what has happened to me quite often. To think that two little pieces of plastic could provide so much opportunity amazes me. One time early on, at a party, a friend asked me, so what else do you do? I looked at him and said, this is it, knowing that I had been traveling the country doing trade shows and TV shows and trekking to Europe promoting my two little pieces of plastic and making quite a living as a result. Being humble, I don't like to brag about what is possible, but the truth is, sometimes we can earn what others deem a full year's salary, in a single television appearance.

Having the opportunity to go to England and Germany to continue my successful journey was like finding money in your jeans pocket when doing laundry, especially since they called us. Big-business owners reading this might think nothing of it, but knowing that this all came from nothing is something any small business owner can fully appreciate.

Over there QVC operates a bit differently than in the United States. Although the same high standards are expected, QVC doesn't appear to work at the same urgency as it does here. For example, it takes a little longer to get through the internal processes of quality assurance. Follow-up with buyers is also a laborious process.

Other things, too, need to be accounted for when doing business in Europe. Often, a day can be lost because of the five-hour time difference between our locations. We spend a lot of time trading e-mails as a result. Moreover, shipping the product overseas is a huge time constraint. Getting your product there usually happens by boat, which means it will take four to six weeks in transit, and export paperwork needs to be completed as well. Big businesses likely have someone familiar with the process. For the rest of us, there is a learning curve, but it's not difficult.

One other major difference to consider is in regard to sales. In the United Kingdom, our sales have been about one quarter of our U.S. appearances. From my conversations with others, this seems to be the norm. Also, airtimes in the United Kingdom have been longer and we have seen multiple appearances in one day more frequently than in the United States. The first time we went to England, we had three appearances over two days, and during the same trip, when we hopped over to Germany, we had five appearances over two days.

Combining appearances with the two neighboring countries has been the way we have scheduled our overseas jaunts. This is a big plus, in that our transportation costs and the time spent traveling are less than if we were going to each country straightaway.

When it comes to going on-air, the process is similar to the United States. The hosts are just as professional and the sets and crew are well organized. In the United Kingdom, the process is as smooth as it is in the United States. Germany has a complicating factor, however. It involves another language. For me, this has been handled two different ways. One way involves the host translating directly for me any phone calls we receive or anything the host says that I need to know. This works very well, although it detracts from the flow and pace of the demonstrations. The other way involves a translation directly into my earpiece as it happens. This is quicker, but takes a little time to get used to. I personally wanted the experience of being on-air there with the product, but future plans involve using demonstrators fluent in German.

Lastly, purchase orders have always been in U.S. dollars. Despite the value of the dollar, whether up or down, I prefer not to speculate in other currencies, so, if and when given a choice, I always recommend working in U.S. dollars. This way your purchase order is relative to what your costs are, and what you receive is based on a firm figure and not a future, possibly fluctuating number.

I would summarize the overseas opportunities as having to be individually considered. If the numbers work and you're looking to expand your product's exposure, then it might be a good idea to enter the European market. For us it was, and continues to be, a positive experience.

Building Relationships with Professionals

One time I was scheduled for an overnight on-air appearance. Many of the overnight appearances were preludes to full-day events, so on this day, QVC's idea of fun was to create a slumber party atmosphere for the viewers, complete with pajamas, much to my chagrin.

The green room was alive with the guests and friends of guests. Among them I spotted a new face I hadn't seen. She was sitting on the couch in pajamas and so I introduced myself. She said she was there to support her mother, who was appearing on-air during the overnight. She went on to explain her pajama attire as embracing the spirit of the overnight—plus, she really did roll out of bed for the event.

The ripple effect of this encounter was that this daughter of a guest was a publicist. That evening, she convinced me that I didn't have to be a famous actor to reap the benefits of a publicist, which had been my preconceived notion. As our talks continued, we agreed to work together and in the weeks to follow we outlined a plan.

Flash forward. The chance encounter lead to publicity I never thought possible. She was directly responsible for our appearance on *The Rosie O'Donnell Show* and contributed significantly to our winning the Most Innovative Product Award two times and the Buyer's Choice award for our industry's largest trade show.

She became a major part of our promotions, and I quickly learned the value of her work. On a monetary basis, instead of taking a full-page paid advertisement in a magazine, which is very expensive relatively speaking, we would get multi-page articles written about us for free. Of course, we had her retainer to pay, but it amounted to much less than the full-page ads would have cost.

Need Publicity? Think on Your Feet Like "The Greatest" Did

Ask yourself, what is happening in your surroundings that you can turn into a publicity opportunity? Or, what is happening in current events that you can relate to your product?

Muhammad Ali was doing a photo shoot for *Sports Illustrated* soon after turning pro. During the photo shoot, Ali asked the photographer what other magazines he did work for, and he answered *Life* magazine. When Ali asked him if he could get him in *Life* magazine, which was one of the largest and most popular magazines of the day, the photographer told him that he didn't have a chance.

Ali later asked what other kinds of photos he took, to which the photographer replied that underwater photography was his specialty. Being quick and creative, The Greatest saw his opportunity and threw a colorful jab, "Do you know I'm the only fighter in the world that trains underwater?"

The next day found Ali, for the first time ever, up to his neck in a swimming pool throwing jabs as the photographer snapped images of the champ. The result was a five-page feature in *Life* magazine. If you're creative, quick thinking, and willing to work like The Greatest did, you can get a lot of free publicity.

Articles written about companies or topics that include information on manufacturers and developers come from unbiased parties and so carry more weight than a self-promoted advertisement. This approach not only saved us advertising dollars because we could take smaller ads in support of the articles, but also increased our reputation, exposure, and significantly boosted our sales.

When I think back to my beginnings and my mindset at the time, I really have to be honest and say I never would have thought of pursuing a publicist. My thoughts were that publicists were out of reach, a luxury, but the truth is, publicists are an everyday part of our business efforts to this day and are well worth the expense if you have great products and can stand behind them. The relaxed environment we were in at QVC during the overnight opened the door for me to learn from a very successful one that I might otherwise not have met.

Gaining Expert Status

The last thing I will add in this chapter about open doors ties together a lot of things covered in this book. Being a guest on QVC helps position you as an expert in your field. In fact, nothing propels you to expert status faster than appearing on a national television show. And once you are recognized as an expert in your field, you can capitalize on this stature by broadening your reach.

You can offer yourself to print media and increase the exposure of your business. You can offer yourself to any of the major morning television shows for special segments where they need an expert about any given topic for any given piece they are working on. You can become a professional demonstrator for other company's products. You can represent other people's products as an agent and introduce them to QVC, as I often do. You can write articles, books, and literally begin a consulting business in a variety of capacities.

The possibilities are endless for you to tie together your status as an expert with expanding your reach as a business and as an individual. Keep your eyes and ears open for all the opportunities that become available once you appear on QVC.

Being fortunate enough to make it to QVC is a feat in itself, but what you do with the opportunity can accelerate everything you hope to achieve for your product and your business faster than you can imagine.

CHAPTER

17

Beyond QVC—The Big Picture

I watch the inventor shows on television. I go to trade shows and meet start-up and established businesses of all types. The picture I consistently see when it comes to small businesses or sole inventors is the same as when I look at the individual that is part of a large company. Product developers, creative types, people of all kinds are driven by their ideas. Many of the people I meet are driven to change and impact lives, whether they know it or not.

I was just a boy when I first started coming up with ideas that could solve problems. I remember sitting in fifth grade in the spring time. The windows were open and a breeze was blowing. At the same time, school was almost over for the day, so I was thinking about my classroom chore for that week—cleaning those same dusty blinds, which by now were turning my tranquil daydream into a jarring experience as the growing breeze smacked them against the windows.

Then, in an instant I was lost again, thinking about how to solve the problem of the clanging blinds and about my cleaning of them. I imagined two panes of glass, with an airtight seal, the blinds being between the panes of glass with an external handle you could twist to open and close them. In my young mind, I saw it all, clear as can be. The blinds would never again bang in the wind or get dirty. Being a child, I didn't think any more of it, nor did I take any action to make it a reality once the bell rang. I simply cleaned them and went on my way.

More than twenty years later, I saw this very invention being offered on television by Pella Windows and thought how right it was and how it really could make life easier for a lot of people. But it was with the eye of wisdom that I saw its benefit, for at the time I first thought of it, and this is true about my early days of inventing the products I would eventually take to QVC, I wasn't thinking of impact, or higher purpose, for that matter. I was only thinking of making my job easier and my world more peaceful.

It's kind of like the story of many a famous rock star that started a band to meet girls and along the way discovered the music. The big picture is present, and seeing it sooner than later can change the course of your business for the better.

I share with you a string of pivotal points in my life as a product creator that helped me understand my own journey because I believe it will help you find and/or validate your own. The experiences helped me to find purpose and focus, two things that I have found to be essential in getting through the obstacles that can sometimes prevent people from attaining their dreams.

Several years ago, at a jam-packed consumer convention, a woman made her way through the crowd toward our demonstration table. It was a hot day in the middle of May in Puyallup, Washington, and it was hotter inside the building because the owners had yet to turn on the air-conditioning system.

As the woman approached the table I noticed that she was wearing gloves! I was in the middle of demonstrating our Kreate-a-lope® envelope templates to a group of about 50 onlookers crowding the edge of my table. As I neared the end of the demonstration, the point at which people would have the opportunity to purchase the templates, the gloved woman started to speak.

"Are you the inventor of the Kreate-a-lope®?" she asked.

"Yes," I answered.

"I belong to a group of crafters that does crafts for therapy," she said.

Usually, at this point in the demo people ask questions specific to the templates, so I was taken aback by her interruption. Also, I was a little upset, because I had yet to finish the demonstration for the crowd that had been watching, and it was right at the point where I would make the sale by announcing the price and the special offer we created for the show, which I thought was the reason I was there—to sell templates.

But she continued. "I belong to a group, we all have the same condition, and we find crafts to be great therapy for us, and I just wanted to say thank you." She motioned to her gloves.

The woman was fairly young. I really didn't know what to think because she couldn't have been older than forty. "How bad could it be?" I thought to myself as I looked at her covered hands. She saw me looking but she was not uncomfortable. Then she asked if I would like to see her hands. I nodded and she pulled one of them back over her fingers to reveal a very swollen hand.

She said, "Until we found the Kreate-a-lope®, it was very difficult for us to make envelopes that matched our cards. You see, most of us can't use scissors because we suffer from a very rare type of arthritis. I have strength in my hands, even though they're very swollen. So I can grip paper okay, which is why we can use your templates."

It was the first time I saw the true impact of something I once struggled to bring to market. I saw a bigger picture, and it was the ripple effect of my decisions and the actions taken to follow my instincts.

I've never felt like I was the inventor of many of my inventions. I do, however, feel that I am "the manager" of them and have a responsibility to share them with people. Being able to see and hear how important they could be to someone like the woman with arthritis began to change my perspective on things.

Another time, I went to California to do another consumer trade show. This was very early on in my business. I arrived a few days before the show because I wanted to visit a few stores before the event.

There was one particular store that I wanted to visit because it was one of the first stores in the country to carry our then-unknown templates. I had sent an introductory letter to the owner before my very first appearance on QVC, and she ordered 125 templates from us after seeing it on TV. She sold them all in the first weekend by simply demonstrating them to everyone who walked in the store.

I wanted to introduce myself to her in person to thank her for taking a chance with us. She was in the middle of telling me a story about one of her customers that loved our product when the front door to the store opened. She turned to me and said, "In fact, here comes one of your biggest fans now."

After being introduced, the customer began to speak. "I want to thank you for developing this wonderful invention and for sharing it with the crafting community," she said. "You see it's the first envelope template I ever had success with using because it shows me where to align my rubber-stamped images."

Now, to anyone that has ever used one of our Kreate-a-lopes®, this comment may not seem unusual because the templates contain a number of helpful markings to help align images. But the extraordinary thing about this woman, and her comment in particular, was that she was blind. She used our envelope template and her rubber stamps by feel!

As we spoke, she pulled out some of her samples. I was transfixed. They were stunning. One of them was the most brilliant sunset I had ever seen in art form. Another was a small deer in a wooded area nuzzling its mother.

I came to learn that the woman had lost her sight at a young age, so she had a memory of shapes and their colors, and somehow she was able to assemble the most amazing works of art without being able to see!

She told me how her friends and family loved to receive her creations and mentioned how she recently began to sell many of her unsent cards and envelopes for charity! She showed me how she felt the shapes of her stamps and described what she "saw" as her hand moved over one of her favorite ones that she had in her large—a purse so large and so full of supplies I would have thought she was about to open her own store.

My new friend and I talked for over an hour that day. When I finally had to leave, it was as a changed person. From that day forward, I truly understood the gift I was given when the idea for the Kreate-a-lope® first came to me.

To be the recipient of a once-stranger's gratitude when I considered myself merely the conduit for my inventions was more than I ever expected. But as wonderful as that experience was, it was only the first of many similarly blessed encounters that continue to allow us to appreciate our lives and to keep trying to create great products.

We're not saving lives, but we're having an impact. You might be the one with the life-saving device, and I hope you see the big picture that is beyond monetary success. There is a reason you have your ideas, or have become involved with someone else's. Keep moving, keep creating, and keep making things happen.

Final Thoughts

Congratulations! You made it through!

You didn't hesitate to buy this book—now don't hesitate to take action. If your product needs a tweak to make it a viable contender for QVC's audience, then get started. If you have to get help from someone to get to the next level, don't wait. Ask for help. The faster you can get to the door, the sooner you will walk through it.

If you walk away with one thing, let it be this. If you can sell your product to one person, you can likely sell it to millions. As I've said before, the difference is exposure, and QVC might be the launching pad for your brilliant product. If you don't make the moves to get on TV or launch your product in some other way, you might end up spending the rest of your life wondering, "What if?" So, get started.

Remember my niche products that I've spoken about throughout the book. Getting on TV allowed me to skyrocket my business, and it can do the same for you, whether you are just getting started or have been around for a while. Although your journey may be far different, remember to reference this book, but more importantly to follow your instincts, because the waters are always changing. Another thing, don't take no for an answer. Even some of the most successful products have been turned down many times.

I hope this book serves to be a mentor for you, much the same way my real-life mentors helped me. That is precisely the reason I put into words much of my experience. I hope you experience massive successes with your products, and I sincerely want to thank you for taking the time to read the information within.

I also want to applaud you for your courage to move forward. You very likely have a lot of naysayers in your life, or might be encountering obstacles. I'm here to tell you not to pay them much attention. I tell my friends and anyone else that asks, "If you want to

123

make a million dollars, go ask the advice of someone that has made a million dollars." It's that simple. Model success, and you will be successful!

All the best, and good luck to you in all your endeavors,

Nick Romer
www.SellonQ.com

APPENDIX A

Resource Directory

For a complete list of all the marketing and business building resources mentioned in the book, along with hundreds of others, please visit www.SellonQ.com and click on Free Resources for immediate access. The resources listed here are not necessarily endorsements, but are provided as a reference.

Helpful Groups and Organizations

- American Marketing Association, www.ama.org. This is one of the largest professional associations for marketers.
- Ask the Inventors, www.asktheinventors.com. Experienced advice is available for new inventors.
- Electronic Retailing Association (formerly the National Infomercial Marketing Association), www.retailing.org. This is a trade association for companies that use direct response to sell goods and services to the public on television, online and on radio.
- Federal Trade Commission, www.ftc.gov
- Google Patent Search, www.google.com/patents
- Intellectual Property Law Server, www.intelproplaw.com. Information is available about intellectual property law including patent, trademark and copyright.
- International Licensing Industry Merchandisers' Association, www.licensing.org

- MarketingSherpa, www.marketingsherpa.com. This research firm specializes in tracking what works in all aspects of marketing (and what does not.) It is not an agency, consultancy, or other vendor seeking business. Its goal is to give marketers of the world the stats, inspiration, and instructions to improve their results.
- Minnesota Inventor's Congress, www.inventhelper.org. This is a nonprofit organization dedicated to the advancement of inventors.
- National Inventor Fraud Center, www.inventorfraud.com. The Center started with the goal of providing information to consumers about invention promotion companies and how people can market their ideas.
- Small Business Administration, www.sba.gov
- United Inventor's Association, www.uiausa.com
- United States Copyright Office, www.copyright.gov
- United States Patent and Trademark Office, www.uspto.gov
- United States Patent and Trademark Office Resource Center for Inventors, www.uspto.gov/web/offices/com/iip/index.htm

Home Shopping Channels

QVC, www.qvc.com
1200 Wilson Dr.
West Chester, PA 19380
(484) 701-1000
(800) 345-1515

The Home Shopping Network (HSN), www.hsn.com
1 HSN Drive
St. Petersburg, FL 33729
(727) 872-1000
(800) 284-3100

Trade Shows

Just about every industry has at least one major trade show every year. Here is a partial list of conventions and trade shows, along with the sponsoring organizations. The list is far from complete, as there are entire publications dedicated to maintaining this valuable information.

Many libraries have access to resources containing lists of current trade shows and conventions, such as the *Directory of Conventions*, published by *Successful Meetings* magazine, New York, NY.

- Consumer Electronics Show, www.cesweb.org
- Craft & Hobby Association, www.hobby.org
- George Little Management (GLM), www.glmshows.com. GLM is involved in the production of nearly forty trade shows in some fifteen cities across the United States and Canada.
  - ◆ Alberta Gift Show
  - ◆ Boston Gift Show®
  - ◆ Cadeaux™, The Luxury Gift Collection at JCK
  - ◆ California Gift Show®
  - ◆ EX·TRACTS®
  - ◆ Global Home Textiles™
  - ◆ The Gourmet Housewares Show™
  - ◆ HSMAI's Affordable Meetings® Mid-America
  - ◆ HSMAI's Affordable Meetings® National
  - ◆ HSMAI's Affordable Meetings® West
  - ◆ International Contemporary Furniture Fair® (ICFF®)
  - ◆ International Hotel/Motel & Restaurant Show®
  - ◆ Mid Atlantic Cash & Carry Show
  - ◆ Montreal Gift Show
  - ◆ National Stationery Show®
  - ◆ New York Gift Cash & Carry® Show...Gifts to Go
  - ◆ New York Home Textiles Show®
  - ◆ New York International Gift Fair®
  - ◆ Orlando Gift Show®
  - ◆ Portland Gift & Accessories Show
  - ◆ San Francisco International Gift Fair®
  - ◆ The Seattle Gift Show®
  - ◆ SOURCES® LA
  - ◆ The Supply Side®
  - ◆ SURTEX®
  - ◆ Toronto International Gift Fair™

- ◆ Tourist, Resort & Imprinted Products Show
- ◆ Vancouver Gift Show
- International Home & Housewares Show, www.housewares .org/ihshow
- School, Home, & Office Products Association, http://shopa.org
- Trade Show Week, www.directory.tradeshowweek.com/ directory/index.asp. This is a directory of trade shows sortable by industry category, country, province, state, cities, months, keywords, and more.
- Variety Merchandise Show, www.varietymerchandiseshows.com

Trend Tools

http://pages.ebay.com/sellercentral/whatshot.html

www.freekeywords.wordtracker.com

www.google.com/trends

www.trendwatching.com

Manufacturing and Packaging

Freund Container, www.freundcontainer.com. Shipping supplies can be ordered here.

Thomas Register and Thomas Regional Directory of Manufacturers, www.thomasnet.com

Uline, www.uline.com. Shipping supplies can be ordered here.

APPENDIX B

Frequently Asked Questions

Q: How much will QVC order if it accepts my product?

A: This varies, based on product, intended time slot, product category, stature of company, and so on. Generally, for an initial order for a daytime slot, an order will be prepared for $50,000 to $75,000 in retail value. This means that if the item will sell on-air for $25 per unit, then you will have to produce 2,000 units for a $50,000 prep ($50,000 / $25 = 2,000). Once your product is successful thereafter, orders vary greatly, depending on the aforementioned circumstances and QVC's projections.

Q: When do you ship the orders to customers after your air date?

A: You don't ship to customers. In most cases, you ship your order to one of QVC's predesignated warehouses before you go on-air. Generally, your product will be required in the warehouse at least a month before your air date. Only certain products and under certain conditions do you ship directly to consumers. One example of this might be a perishable food product.

Q: How much does it cost to be on QVC?

A: It doesn't cost anything to be on QVC. QVC is free. The only cost and risk to you is the cost involved in manufacturing your product. Plus, you are responsible for your own travel expenses and lodging.

Q: Will QVC replay my airing?

A: No, QVC does not tape any airings. It is a live broadcast 24 hours a day, 364 days a year. It does not broadcast on Christmas Day.

Q: Who pays the freight for product being shipped to QVC?

A: Unless other agreements have been made, the standard policy in the United States is that the manufacturer pays for freight to QVC's warehouse(s). The exception is shipments going to QVC UK or QVC Germany from the United States. This expense is paid for by the respective division.

Q: Does QVC guarantee sales?

A: No, QVC does not guarantee sales.

Q: What does QVC look for in a product?

A: QVC looks for products that answer yes to as many of the following questions as possible, in addition to a number of other factors covered in the book:

- Is your product demonstrable?
- Is your product unique?
- Is your product brand new to the market?
- Does your product solve a common problem?
- Is your product a significant improvement over something already in existence?
- Has your product been successful in other markets?
- Does your product have mass appeal?
- Does your product fit into one of the categories on QVC's Web site?

Q: How do you get on QVC?

A: There are many ways. You can fill out the online form, go to an open call, contact an agent representative, be discovered at a trade show or store, find someone with connections and ask for their help, and more. The many ways are covered within the pages herein.

Q: How can I become a host on QVC?

A: Look for postings on its Web site for upcoming openings. Additionally, QVC will broadcast this information when it is searching for new hosts.

Q: How much will QVC pay me for my idea?

A: Nothing. QVC does not buy ideas. It behaves like a typical retailer and thus looks for finished products to sell to its customers.

Q: How does QVC make money?

A: QVC makes money by buying your product at a discount and selling it at a markup.

Q: If my product is accepted, will QVC train me to sell it on-air?

A: QVC requires all on-air guests to attend a Guest Excellence Seminar at its headquarters in West Chester, Pennsylvania, prior to demonstrating their product on-air. There is no cost to participate, but you will have to pay your travel expenses.

Find detailed answers to all the questions listed here and more inside the pages of this book.

Glossary of Terms

agent—An individual or group that represents product developers.

backorder—When orders are taken for products not in stock but that will be ordered and eventually used to fill the orders taken.

backyard fence selling—A nonthreatening approach to selling where the guest and host converse in a manner akin to having a conversation among neighbors over the backyard fence.

bell curve—A depiction of a normal distribution over time. In terms of a product life cycle, a bell curve looks like a bell and indicates the sales volume of a product over time, including the introduction (rising), the plateau (flattening), and the decline (descending).

boom—A long pole used to hold a microphone or camera.

bounceback—Information in your product that attempts to solicit customers. One example of a bounceback is: "For more information please visit our website, www.GreenSneakers.com."

B-roll—A B-roll is auxiliary video footage prepared in advance used to augment a presentation.

camera pan—Movement of a camera to create a panoramic effect.

close up shot—A camera shot taken in close proximity to the object.

consumer trade show—A convention where companies gather to exhibit and sell products to consumers.

coordinating producer—This is the person that runs the studio floor. He or she communicates and clarifies legal claims for hosts and guests, maintains the production values, and communicates key strategies and points of execution to the live crew. He or she manages guests in the studio and is the liaison between the line producer and the studio floor.

co-venture—A collaboration between two companies in any number of forms to mutual benefit; a large company can offer distribution services to a small company, two companies can combine products to compose one product, and so on.

cross-promote—A method of recommending additional products to a consumer that might be on interest based on their current selection.

deferred payment—A term QVC uses when it allows the customer to pay for an item at a later date. These are made available only to holders of QVC's Qcard.

direct response television—Frequently abbreviated DRTV; marketing of goods and services directly from the manufacturer or wholesaler to the consumer by means of television. Includes infomercials, home shopping channels.

distributor—A company that purchase goods at a deep discount in order to sell direct to retailers or other wholesale companies.

drop ship—The shipping of a product directly from the manufacturer to the customer without requiring inventory carrying by the retailer.

DRTV—See direct response television.

earpiece—An electronic device fitted to one's ear in order to be able to receive communications from the show producer and to hear phone calls during the on-air presentation.

easy pay—A term QVC uses to allow a designated number of payments for an item at no extra charge.

economies of scale—Reduction in cost per unit resulting from increased production due to operational efficiencies. As production increases, economies of scale can be accomplished because the cost of producing each additional unit gets lower.

FCC—Federal Communications Commission (www.fcc.gov). It was created under the U.S. Communications Act of 1934, and its board of commissioners is appointed by the president of the United States. The FCC is a U.S. government agency that regulates interstate and international communications, including wire, cable, radio, TV, and satellite.

FMV—Full motion video/digital imaging. This is where the on-air product shot is created. This is the still photo that QVC uses for any previews and during a presentation.

fulfillment—The shipping of product after an order is placed.

fulfillment house—A third-party company that handles order fulfillment on another company's behalf.

full motion video/digital imaging—See FMV.

green room—A waiting room or lounge for the use of on-air talent and associates.

hair and make-up— On-location hair and make-up stylist provided by QVC, made available for on-air guests.

host promo—A product that is promoted by the host of a given segment. Promos happen prior to airing and throughout the segment.

HSN—The Home Shopping Network.

infomercial—A long commercial generally longer than two minutes providing product information or goods for sale.

introductory price—See IP.

IP—Introductory price of an item selling on QVC that is generally 8 to10 percent lower than the regular price that stays in effect for a predetermined amount of appearances. Not all items are granted an IP.

keystone pricing—A method of setting the price of merchandise for resell to an amount that is double the wholesale price.

laser shot—A static image of a product and/or its contents used to showcase a product on-air. Created by QVC's FMV department.

Lavaliere microphone—A small microphone that can be easily hidden in a piece of clothing so as not to be seen by the camera.

lead time—The time required to manufacture and ship a product in advance of an on-air appearance.

licensing—A general agreement between two parties where one party agrees to allow another party use of their intellectual property; invention, brand item, etc.

line producer—The person that directs all elements of the show.

loss leader—A type of pricing strategy where an item is sold below cost in an effort to stimulate other, profitable sales.

mailers—Promotional literature mailed to prospective customers.

mass market—Items produced for consumption in large quantities.

mass media—The section of the media specifically conceived and designed to reach a very large audience.

master shot—A camera shot that captures the entire piece of dramatic action.

monitor—Display produced by a camera.

networking—The act of making and creating business relationships for mutual benefit.

niche product—A product that is manufactured and marketed for specialized uses.

one shot—An image of a single person generally from the waste up.

one time only—See OTO.

open call—An announcement to meet without an appointment made to the general public.

OTO—One time only; a QVC term to denote a product that will be offered at a special discount for one time. It is an item presented after a today's special value sells out and it is the lowest price the given item will ever appear on QVC.

product dubner—The four lines of text appearing on the television screen that is aired to the public that describes the product being shown.

product pipeline—Any number of products in the same category that are closely related

product showcase—A display found in many trade shows featuring the newest, most innovative, or unique products.

profit margin—A term used to indicate profitability. Determined by dividing net income by revenue.

prototype—A typical example or model of an item that will be manufactured to specifications at a later date.

purchase order—Written authorization for a supplier to ship products at a specified price.

Qcard—A credit card issued exclusively to QVC's customers.

QVC—The home shopping channel whose letters stand for *quality value convenience.*

QVC vendor—An approved vendor that sells directly to QVC.

retail price—The selling price of an item to consumers.

RTV—Return to vendor; product that has been rejected by the customer or the buyer's inspection department and is awaiting shipment back to the supplier

set—The setting composed of furniture and so on where filming takes place.

SKU—Stock keeping unit—a number or identifier assigned to keep track of a product.

social proof—A phenomenon that occurs when any of number of people cannot make a decision and elect to make choices based on the assumption that others are better informed.

static shot—A stationary image of a product.

studio operations desk—A central hub of activity in the QVC studio that handles any number of coordinated activities such as preparing guests and hosts with electronics, providing scheduling information, keeping track of guests, facilitating documents, etc.

suggested retail price—A suggestion for pricing a product to consumers made by the manufacturer.

surge—When your product sells out and more than the normal amount of backorders are taken because your product was selling so quickly. These orders are taken when the manufacturer is capable of producing the item quickly or has the inventory in stock and ready to ship.

T-call—A phone call received by a customer that has used or previously purchased an item that is taken live on-air.

testimonial call— See T-call.

today's special value—See TSV.

trade show—A convention where manufacturers gather to exhibit their product to perspective wholesale customers.

TSV—Today's special value; a QVC term given to an item that is showcased in multiple airings on a given day, beginning with a midnight kickoff and lasting until 11:59 p.m., or until quantities last.

TV sales manager—The person in charge of discussing anything from sales strategies to broadcasting logistics with the on-air guest as well as arrival times.

two shot—A camera shot of two people, usually from the waist up.

upsell—The process or method of selling an additional product that is related to the primary product that is offered to the buyer while they are still on the telephone purchasing the main item.

vendor bounceback—See bounceback.

wholesale—Selling or pertaining to selling goods in large quantities at a discount for resale to the consumer

About the Author

Nick Romer (Basking Ridge, New Jersey) is an award-winning inventor of over a hundred products developed for crafters and hobbyists. He has appeared on QVC in the United States for more than 14 years, and his products have been featured on many other shows, including QVC United Kingdom, QVC Germany, The Shopping Channel Canada, *The Rosie O'Donnell Show, Good Morning Philadelphia*, and *Good Morning Arizona*. He is a recipient of QVC's Million Dollar Sales Award, a two-time winner of Primedia's Award of Excellence, and has also won the Craft and Hobby Association Buyer's Choice Award. His innovations have been sold in more than 22,000 stores in 23 countries and can be found on his Web sites, www.GreenSneakers.com and www.ScrapWow.com. As a business strategist and product development specialist, he has helped countless others pursue their dreams as well.

Index

FREE Gifts Linked to This Book

To help you get maximum value from this book,
I have reserved a collection of

<u>FREE</u> Bonus Resources and Audios—a $497 Value

that are waiting for you.

- **FREE Audios** . . . extension of this book – enroll today!

- **FREE E-Mail Course . . .** 7 part course designed to help you take immediate steps toward realizing your dreams.

- **FREE Bonus Materials** . . . a surprise package of pure content and every other extra resource referred to throughout this book.

Claim Your **<u>FREE</u>** Resources right now while it's fresh in your mind. Follow these 2 easy steps:

Step 1. Go to this URL:

www.SuccessOnQ.com/purchased

Step 2. Authenticate

You will be prompted to open the book to a certain page and find a particular word. This is our way of verifying that you purchased the book.